Monetary Governance in Search of New Space

About the Author

Asuri Vasudevan is currently Special Adviser to the Governor, Central Bank of Nigeria on Monetary Policy & Operations. Prior to holding this position, he was on a 3-year IMF assignment (2006-2009) at the same Bank. His major previously-held positions were: Executive Director, Reserve Bank of India (1996-2000) and Adviser to the Executive Director for India at the International Monetary Fund, Washington DC (1984-1989). He was member of India delegations to the IMF-WB meetings between 1984 and 1989 and 1993-2000. He was member of the two Task Forces relating to International Standards and Codes of the erstwhile Financial Stability Forum at Bank for International Settlements (BIS), Basle. His book *Central Banking for Emerging Market Economies* (Academic Foundation, 2003) has received acclaim as an important contribution to understanding of modern central banking. His previous books were on deficit financing (based on PhD thesis) and strategy of development planning. He has edited books on external debt and money and banking, and has several articles on monetary and development policy issues.

Monetary Governance in Search of New Space

Emerging Market Economy Perspectives

A. VASUDEVAN

ACADEMIC FOUNDATION
NEW DELHI

www.academicfoundation.com

First published in 2012
by

ACADEMIC FOUNDATION
4772-73 / 23 Bharat Ram Road, (23 Ansari Road),
Darya Ganj, New Delhi - 110 002 (India).
Phones : 23245001 / 02 / 03 / 04.
Fax : +91-11-23245005.
E-mail : books@academicfoundation.com
www.academicfoundation.com

Cataloging in Publication Data--DK
Courtesy: D.K. Agencies (P) Ltd. <docinfo@dkagencies.com>

Vasudevan, A., 1940-
Monetary governance in search of new space : emerging market economy perspectives / A. Vasudevan.
p. cm.
Includes bibliographical references (p.) and index.
ISBN 13: 9788171889297
ISBN 10: 8171889298

1. Monetary policy. 2. Capital market. 3. Banks and banking, Central. 4. Globalization--Economic aspects. I. Title.

DDC 332.46 23

Typeset by Italics India, New Delhi.
Printed and bound in India.

10 9 8 7 6 5 4 3 2 1

Contents

Foreword

It is a great pleasure and an honour for me to present this book on *Monetary Governance in Search of New Space: Emerging Market Economy Perspectives* written by a friend, colleague, and my adviser on monetary policy—Dr A. Vasudevan for the academic community, policymakers and the general public at large. The book unravels the mystery of monetary governance principles and practices in emerging market economies. It represents a valuable contribution to a topic in the field of monetary theory that is scantly articulated in the literature, which only a professional researcher/economist and a master of the subject such as Vasudevan, will venture to undertake. His vast wealth of knowledge garnered from his days as central bank researcher-cum-academic in India and as Advisor to the Executive Director for India at the International Monetary Fund (IMF) has been brought to bear in the writing of this veritable information bank, in lucid style and with remarkable clarity of thinking.

The book could be regarded as an update to his previous book titled *Central Banking for Emerging Market Economies* published in 2003, with nuanced and strong emphasis on issues of governance at both the national and international levels. Vasudevan identifies the features that make monetary governance ineffective such as macro-economic imbalances and high unemployment rate. He emphatically noted that the problems of poor monetary governance could be accentuated by changes in global economic linkages and liberalisation as well as domestic economic and political conditions. He then discusses every important aspect of sound monetary governance in detail with coverage of conceptual issues, institutional requirements, the rainbow of interests, analytics and communications, international dimension and the way forward. In chapter 3 of the book for instance, discussions on rainbow of interests capture various jurisdictions where conflicts of interests could arise, particularly in the execution of the responsibilities of principal actor and agent which could culminate into what Vasudevan refers to as 'game-theoretic mode'. In such a situation, the attainment of the common good by the authorities would become difficult. The book advocates harmonisation of interests of fiscal and monetary authorities to create macroeconomic stability and policy certainty as critical for price stability as well as high sustainable growth. In addition, it underscores the need to address the supervisory and regulatory structure and ring fence the financial system with tighter norms through Basle III regulations.

The experiences of countries such as China and India that addressed to a significant extent the effects of the Asian and the recent global financial crisis through the adoption of capital controls have been cited as helpful examples. The book also notes that Canada was not affected owing to the establishment of a supervisory and regulatory structure that ensured market discipline, the absence of which was at the heart of the recent global financial crisis. However, as the book argues, there are some areas that require more insights by the monetary authority and other regulators in the financial system. First, there is the need to investigate the empirical relationship between regulation and growth. Second, what has prevented the authorities from investigating why the regulations in place were not complied with and why was the whistle not blown for non-compliance and the appropriate actions taken? Third, there is currently no clear view on whether financial institutions that are in severe financial stress should be bailed out or provided with the fence of forbearance without any conditions and costs and burdens to the society at large.

The book elucidates some measures that need to be put in place to enhance monetary governance. These include thorough and constant monitoring of processes and market intelligence to achieve sound and seamless monetary governance in every evolving institution within the financial system. The coordination of actions of the participants in the financial markets and real sector through effective surveillance and regulatory mechanisms coupled with the conduct of macroprudential oversight is deemed to be critical in facilitating effective and efficient monetary governance. The author alludes to the view that emerging and developing countries require more vigilance to guard against financial instability and uncertainty, as it may be more difficult for these economies to recover in the event of any financial crisis owing to their weak economic base.

His thoughts on the institutional requirements for monetary governance set the book apart from his past writings. Here, he advocates a decentralised institutional mechanism which contains built-in-checks that allow monetary and fiscal policy committee members to have views of their own, and guard against possible collusion by committee members and authorities. He calls for the rotation of the membership of the Committees every other year. This option differs from the collegial-oriented approach which usually reflects the views of the authorities, sieved from speeches and interviews of senior government and central bank officials before the dates of the policy committee meetings. Vasudevan stresses that the rules and processes needed by institutions and the legal framework required should be clearly defined and properly understood by those who are going to implement the decisions.

It is a pleasure to see references in the book to Africa, and in particular to Nigeria. The book is a delight to read and the key messages focus on the need for the enforcement of accountability, structural reforms and knowledge-centric information management by central banks and other government authority. These are essential for the appropriate design of monetary and financial policies that are most relevant for financial stability, sustainable economic growth and development. I enjoyed the intellectual wizardry of the author and I recommend the book as a must read for all central bankers, academics, public analysts and postgraduate students of monetary and development economics.

— Sanusi Lamido Sanusi, CON

Governor
Central Bank of Nigeria

Logging In

This book was conceived and almost wholly written in 2010 on my return to India from an international assignment. Before I could finalise the drafts of my writing, my laptop crashed. Fortunately, I did store much of the drafts in my flash drive. Before I could finalise the drafts on my newly acquired laptop, I got another international assignment. I began to work on the drafts over the weekends and on my travels abroad ever since. It almost took 12 months to finalise the work.

The idea behind this work came when I met a few ordinary people on the streets of Mumbai, Hyderabad, Chennai and Delhi and interacted with them regarding their views on the policies of the central bank of the country and of the Federal (Union) government in general. The reactions I received were, not unsurprisingly, unfavourable to the authorities. This was so despite the fact that the country (India) was regarded in international circles as a remarkable economic success, a story that has been made more exciting by situating it in the environs of a difficult and complex democracy. However, those who are familiar with the Indian economic scene from the early days of planned development in the 1950s know that cynicism in general has been there right from the early 1960s till the early part of the 1990s when there took place a shift in the policy regime. The cynicism thereafter continued in varying degrees in many quarters. I believe that cynicism about public policies is not unique only in India: it is commonly seen in other developing countries as well. But what was more disconcerting to me was that even the somewhat better educated among those I met for their views on public policies, were uniformly sceptical of the ability of the authorities to tackle the problems of price rises and unemployment on an enduring basis. The challenge, to good many of them, was clearly one of governance.

Governance is required in all areas of human endeavour. The general public prizes it and wants it to be 'good'. The moment it is perceived to be not good, policymakers are placed under stress to justify their actions. Unfortunately, clear communication of the rationale of public policies will not be enough to satisfy the vast mass of people. Governance is about delivery, not merely dependent on the quality of communication. And it can be decomposed into different parts.

Monetary governance deals with governance through sound macroeconomic policies just as political governance deals with political aspects of society. It has national as well as international dimensions. They both interact in this globalised world of economic business as well as ideas.

At the moment, there is dissonance in the economic trends—growth and inflation—in the two broad groups of countries, the industrial economies and emerging and developing economies. But unemployment and highly inequitable income distribution are common in both the country groups. There are other common elements too, as for example, fiscal imbalances. These challenges are at this point in time quite serious. So long as they exist, monetary governance, irrespective of the group to which a country belongs, will be under stress and could be complicated by domestic political economy considerations as well as by the fact of global economic and financial integration.

The book does not pretend to provide answers. It states the elements that need to be set in place to improve monetary governance. Most of them are not unknown but somehow they seem to be tucked in our subconscious being. They need to be revisited, perhaps frequently. The emerging and developing countries will have to be much more mindful of the challenges they face in this regard partly because the economic base on which they are situated is not strong enough to help them to recover quickly should they falter in their efforts to develop and grow.

The perspectives of emerging market economies on monetary governance principles and practices are not much articulated in the literature. Only in very recent years, some of these perspectives emerging from the writings of analysts from emerging countries and of those in advanced economies whose interests are to some extent biased towards emerging countries, have gained relatively wider support than the viewpoints of other developing countries. But surely, a number of developing countries would graduate into emerging country status sooner than apparent. This book therefore attempts to give the perspectives that are relevant to the entire wide world of emerging and developing countries.

This book may be regarded as an update though brief with an added emphasis on operational and institutional aspects of many of the analytical strands of thinking on central banking that have been elaborated upon in my earlier work, *Central Banking for Emerging Market Economies*, brought out by Academic Foundation, New Delhi in 2003.

This book is dedicated to the memory of late Mr Jonnalagadda Suryanarayana Sarma (J.S. Sarma), one time Economic and Statistical Adviser to the Government of India, Ministry of Food and Agriculture, for lavishing on me and my family enormous affection and for giving me unstinted professional support in all my endeavours right from 1960 to his last day in October 2010. I am beholden to him.

I am sincerely grateful to Mr Sanusi Lamido Sanusi, Governor of the Central Bank of Nigeria, for writing the foreword to the book, despite his heavy work schedule. He is one of the very few central bankers who blazed a new trail in central banking in Africa by focussing on growth, price stability and stability of financial institutions and markets and by placing emphasis on economic and financial governance.

— A. Vasudevan

Blog-logue

(With Apologies to Bloggers and Prologue Lovers)

Take a poll at a public place in any urban area of an emerging economy on a question that teased many economists since about 2007. The question posed for the poll is simple: how do you consider the performance of central banks since the beginning of the 21st century?

To help the common person in the street, the pollsters gave four options to choose with scores ranging from 1 to 5.

Option (a): Not good but hopeful of better policies to be taken

Option (b): Very ordinary

Option (c): Totally wrong and disastrous

Option (d): Good

Each of the four options was given equal weights in the scheme of things. None of the possibilities was defined but each of them is explained in general terms for easy understanding of the common woman.

Not good: While policies have not been as effective as originally anticipated, there is a hope of improved effectiveness, if the challenges are addressed expeditiously and in a sound manner.

Very ordinary: Policy effectiveness is extremely limited since the horses have already bolted out.

Totally wrong: The policies are ineffective and unfair and hence are disapproved.

Good: Policies are effective and if there are perceptions of monetary policies being not as effective as desired, it is because of lack of support from other policies.

The pollsters added: Score 1: 20 per cent; Score 2: 40 per cent; Score 3: 60 per cent; Score 4: 80 per cent and Score 5: 100 per cent.

The pollsters ended the information sheet with a remark: do not write your opinions—just give the scores.

Do this exercise or an exercise akin to it in your own study rooms and if possible in your organisations and find out the results. Let us compare the notes with what would emerge from intuitive reasoning.

What could be the probable outcomes of the intuitive reasoning? Let there be guesses based on the premise that the common woman in the street is intelligent and down-to-earth. She looks at her family budgets very closely. She asks herself a number of questions: have the family budgets faced as severe constraints in the pre-2000 period as at present? She also tries to figure out how certain policies—such as the interest rate changes—have improved her incomes or contained inflation of the goods she normally consumes. She wonders about 'open mouth' operations of central banks as well as of finance ministers and other finance authorities of the government. She knows about the taxes she has to pay but she works out her current disposable income with the one she enjoyed in the period prior to the 21st century. She understands what the poll means but she believes that she has one potent weapon with which she can deal with the authorities in power: the vote. She can destabilise the current government, if she chooses. But she is aware of the limitations of her single vote. She has to go with others in society and do what she wants to achieve. She knows that there will be any number of people who would like to fool her by bribes to win her vote and to win votes of the vast majority of the voting public. Mind you, she might take the bribe, not because she is lured by it but because she knows that along with the bribe there is a threat to her life should she reject it openly. She bemoans the absence of good civil and responsible organisations that act as trustees of society. She decides to vote in accordance with the 'collective conscience' of the society at large.

This is the quintessential modern day woman in democracies in emerging countries and perhaps in most developing countries as well. She will closely examine the options given by the pollsters. She will not vote for options (c) or (d). She will probably settle for (a) or (b). This is a difficult decision to make. Even if she settles for one of the two, she still will have to give a score.

Her dilemma is not *sui generis.* It pervades all common persons and serious economic analysts all over the world. Intuitively speaking, the probability of option (a) obtaining a score above (3), i.e., 60 per cent, is doubtful just as the probability of option (b) scoring above (2), i.e., 40 per cent, is remote. The tie between the options (a) and (b) is thus ruled out. Yet, it is a wonder how the world has not witnessed sharp public protests and demonstrations, if not riots in recent years over the high unemployment in industrialised economies (IEs) and over the high inflation along with slowdown in growth in emerging market economies (EMEs). This has been so, at least till October 2011, notwithstanding the 'occupy Wall Street' demonstrations which have been directed originally against the huge disparity in the pay receipts between those who work in the financial institutions and those working in production of goods and services. The authorities seemed to have got a reprieve: they have to now get their act right and in quick time. Otherwise, there could be sharp societal polarisation leading to overhaul of political regimes.

Many would point out that the above public or opinion poll experiment is too simplistic. There will also be suggestions for making it more substantive. Hard core central bankers will point out that if a poll is taken about the performance of government policies, the outcome would turn out to be far worse. This view is understandable since the public's focus will be on governments on a daily basis partly because governments are elected or selected by the public for the good of the people and when the public perception is that the governments have not delivered on what they were expected to, there will be resentment and apathy that could well border on revolt. The point to note here is that irrespective of the fact that the poll is limited or broad-based in scope, the outcome as we have seen above is essentially illustrative of the societies in which we live. Our experiment, limited as it is, conveys a message that the space hitherto utilised for policy is no longer relevant. Information deficiencies and asymmetries in a world that is increasingly integrated have been substantial and unfortunately intangible. They, together with absence of transparency of policy processes, created financial crisis in the first instance and ultimately the economic crisis. The prevalence of information asymmetries and the lack of transparency have been described in a very placid way as 'market failure'. Markets, however, consist of individuals, institutions and processes with each of them influenced by human mind. Markets do not fail without human intervention of the kind that very few would approve.

There was a belief at least till the financial and economic crisis erupted in 2007/08 that adoption of international standards and codes based on the so-called financial market practices as they exist in IEs would take care of 'market failures'. The work for the evolution of the international standards and codes started around the end of the 20th century soon after the Asian crisis of 1997, which represented a watershed in the modern day literature on governance in financial and economic matters. The Asian crisis originated in Thailand and enveloped a number of Asian nations such as Indonesia, the Philippines, Hong Kong, Korea, Malaysia, and to an extent Japan partly due to economic and financial linkages within the region. It is this spillover effect that led policymakers in most IEs and the multilateral financial institutions such as the International Monetary Fund (IMF) and the World Bank (WB) to first identify the countries that could be considered as major players in the international monetary and financial system. Their efforts culminated in the evolution of the Group of Twenty (G-20) countries as 'systemically important'.[1] The G-20 thus formed is much larger than the smaller groups of IEs such as the Group of Five (G-5), Group of Eight (G-8) and Group of Ten (G-10).

The initial discussions in G-20 and in the international financial community in general seem to have led to the recognition of the idea of working out mechanisms that would bring about a standardised financial discipline the world over. Towards this end, the then Financial Stability Forum (FSF) located in Basle at the Bank for International Settlements (BIS) along with the IMF and WB were assigned the task of generating international standards and codes and the practices in major areas of finance. A report prepared under the auspices of the FSF with Andrew Sheng as the chairperson in 1999/2000 recommended international standards and codes in 12 areas on the assumption that the standards and codes as said to have been practised then in IEs are well established and are conducive to optimal functioning of financial systems. A follow up report under the chairmanship of Axel Nawrath in 2000 gave an idea of the market incentives needed to ensure that the recommended standards and codes are set in all the member countries of the IMF and WB.[2] The G-20 and the multilateral financial institutions have in general accepted the main thrust and message of the reports.

The IMF-WB combine, however, pursued the agenda of promoting the international market practices and standards in EMEs with missionary zeal right away with periodic financial sector assessments in Article IV missions and supplemented in some cases by special technical missions. This zeal however was not shown in the case of IEs since it was believed that the best practices are already well entrenched in these economies. While countries like the UK, concerned about the adverse criticism of asymmetric treatment of members of the IMF-WB, agreed voluntarily to have financial sector assessments, the US did not encourage it till the onset of the financial crisis in 2007/08.[3] In retrospect, the limited assessments made in IEs do not give confidence to economic agents that they were rigorous and robust, as the financial bankruptcies and stresses of a number of financial institutions were uncovered by 2008.

It is unfortunate that neither academic economists nor those in policymaking bodies made any concrete attempts to bring out analytical and empirical works to even highlight the risks in blindly accepting the infallibility of the market practices of standards and codes in IEs. It is this extraordinary silence that seemed to have given rise to the sowing of seeds of financial stress and instability in IEs. All that mattered to the multilateral institutions and to the decision-makers in IEs is to ensure that the spillover and contagion effects of market failures in any one systemically important country are contained by adopting the standards and codes in countries that do not have self-imposed market discipline.

The events leading to the global financial and economic crisis beginning the middle of 2007 show that complacency together with absence of thorough and regular monitoring of market place realities has been at the heart of the matter. Monetary authorities in the US, supposed to be immunised from 'irrational exuberance' a' la Alan Greenspan but eclectic in their approach to the conduct of policy were the first to show complacency, generating in the process the housing bubble. The US Fed and the US Securities and Exchange Commission (SEC) complicated matters by not fully grasping the underlying pitfalls of universal banking. In concert with the Fed, the US Treasury too committed the folly of downing the shutters of the

Lehman Brothers in September 2008, thereby triggering a near-run on the banking industry as a whole. Credit squeeze followed as a result. Countries exposed to the US financial sector elsewhere in the world, in particular other IEs, were quickly wounded. The financial crisis first started in the US quickly became global. When as a consequence growth fell and unemployment increased in the IEs, there was the inevitable global economic crisis. The global crisis proved that there is considerable trade and financial integration between the IEs and the EMEs. This was so unlike the Asian crisis which was relatively region-centric in its impact. It only shows that market participants do not necessarily practice what they recommend as standards to others to follow. Their failed conduct was at the root of the market failures and is a cause for the enormous pains that societies had to undergo all over the globe. This does not mean that the crisis should be seen as an excuse for throwing capitalism out. Nor should capitalism be considered as one that has the inherent characteristic of financial market failure.[4]

The recent crisis has however opened a window of opportunity for governments and central banks to search for new space for policies and their implementation in order to promote vital national interests without jeopardising the interests of the rest of the world. This is a huge responsibility, calling for improving, among others, monitoring processes and market intelligence-gathering and for evolving institutions for sound, seamless monetary governance.

End Notes

1. G-20 consists of the following: Argentina, Australia, Brazil, Canada, China, France, Germany, India, Indonesia, Italy, Japan, Mexico, Russia, Saudi Arabia, South Africa, Korea, Turkey, UK, USA, European Union which is rotated by Council Presidency and ECB. Managing director, IMF and president of the WB, chairman of the International Monetary and Financial Committee, chairman of the Development Committee attend the G-20 meetings on ex-officio basis.
2. The reports by the groups chaired by Andrew Sheng and Axel Nawrath are on the website of the Bank of International Settlements. The titles of the reports are the following: *The Task Force on Implementation of Standards* (Chairman:

Andrew Sheng) and *The Task Group on Incentives to Foster Implementation of Standards and Codes* (Chairman: Axel Nawrath), both of the Financial Stability Forum (then housed in BIS, Basle), 1999 and 2000 available on the website of the BIS.

3. The executive boards of the IMF and World Bank represent member countries numbering 184 in all. The Articles of Agreement stipulate the required majority of the votes cast for decisions to be finally adhered to depending on the subject. For instance, quota increase in the IMF cannot take place unless 85 per cent of the total votes are in favour of it. With regard to the IMF borrowing from members under specified agreements, the requisite majority is only 70 per cent. A simple majority is all that is required when a country seeks a waiver for non-performance of a criterion set under an arrangement. The different gradations in voting majority also mean that developing countries will have to depend on the help of some developed countries simply because developing countries as a group command little over one-third of the total votes of all the members. Even though developing countries do not have majority, the Fund cannot be, according to the Articles, asymmetric in treatment as for example in the case of conditionality.

4. An interesting quote attributed to Alan Blinder is that capitalism without market failures is like religion without sin. This was said to have been made in defence of the Fed at the height of the financial crisis in 2008. While the quote sounds lively, it represents in retrospect a cynical view since many of those in less developed countries living in utter poverty and degradation had to pay high price for the acts of commission of those who, despite best education and economic status, are responsible for the crisis.

1

The Meaning and Content

What should be the content of monetary governance that the common person on the street desires? Is it mere repetition of the age-old objectives of monetary and fiscal policies, such as, illustratively speaking, the maintenance of price stability and promotion of employment/output growth? Or, should one say that it has to be more broad-based in that it should envelop not only what is often referred to as 'financial stability' but also the overarching idea of inclusiveness?[1]

Monetary governance, as the expression denotes, is drawn from the general idea of governance. It is more specific than the commonly found references in the economic literature to 'economic governance' and 'global monetary governance'. To understand the essence of monetary governance, one has to first delineate what economic governance means. Economic governance, according to Avinash Dixit, consists of a number of organisations and actions needed for 'good' functioning of markets, most notably protection of property rights, enforcement of contracts and provision of physical and informational–infrastructure services that are often provided by governments to a large extent without excluding the possibility of the private sector providing such services.[2] Good market functioning thus defined would imply that in the absence of the three major services, there will be economic frictions. The word, 'good' here may not necessarily be the same as optimal and the word, 'services', too broad-based as it appears, could well be considered as conditions for relatively well-functioning markets.

It is clear that the organisations required for the specified services would include central banks and other financial regulators. These organisations would be linked with some of the actions mentioned by Dixit. The point to note here is that 'actions' required for good market functioning cited by Dixit are not merely illustrative but also critical: they would in fact include the real sector with an international interface as well as the financial sector, both at home and cross-border areas.

The expression, monetary governance may therefore be viewed as consisting essentially of institutional mechanisms and processes that are required for the functioning of the tasks that devolve constitutionally on governments as well as on central banks which are assigned certain objectives through legislative enactments. The institutional mechanisms would have to be evolved to formulate as well as to implement the policies laid down for the attainment of specified or implicitly stated objectives.

Monetary governance, so described, is not 'financial governance'. However, one can consider them as close cousins. Financial governance would cover not only the macroeconomic managers but also other organisations that are concerned with the working of the financial sector. Distinguishing monetary governance from financial governance is important because it helps one to understand the nuances of the functional jurisdictions of different participants in the overarching area of the financial sector. Macroeconomic management would be the important functional task of the areas covered by monetary governance. On the other hand, the area of portfolio management and asset distribution undertaken within the context of the principles and policies laid down by macroeconomic managers would be covered under financial governance. Financial governance thus would cover not only the Ministry of Finance/Treasury and the central bank but also organisations that deal with supervision/ monitoring and regulation of markets in securities, insurance, pensions, housing finance, to name a few.

Asset distribution and portfolio management, however, are influenced by the extent and costs of financial intermediation and fiscal incentives. Assets could be both financial and 'real' or physical. Activities in financial and real assets cannot take place on their own: there will inevitably be use of 'money' in its broad sense. The distribution of assets among the different economic agents will affect income flows among the sectors, reflecting in part the position of the relative prices or rates of return. The resulting differences in the growth of the sectors will in turn have effects on commodity prices and asset prices, requiring macroeconomic management to come to the fore. This is the area where monetary governance is always put to severe test.

Macroeconomic management, however, would be ineffective and could even fail if there is no coordination of actions of the participants in different financial and real markets through definitive surveillance and regulatory mechanisms. In other words, financial stability is necessary for price stability, not necessarily the other way around as economists with strong commitment to inflation targetting believed.[3] It is also required for sustainable growth to succeed. This does mean that it is not enough that some major financial institutions are healthy. The entire financial sector has to be healthy at all times. The complex interrelations in the financial sector (markets, institutions) could be disruptive at times. It is therefore necessary to keep in view the reality of the paradox of the fallacy of composition. Microprudential supervision and regulatory mechanisms should be supplemented by macroprudential policies and judgments. The analytics and conduct of macroprudential oversight is a great facilitator of good monetary governance.

End Notes

1. In some countries many objectives are underscored as the ones which governments should address. For example, they may refer to balance of payments stability and optimal income as necessary objectives in addition to growth and price stability. In reality, however, growth can be qualified with certain caveats or elements and could include financial stability as a necessary condition of growth. And price stability could be defined to include commodity prices and exchange rates.

2. Economic governance as a subject covers a vast field and cannot be easily distinguished from the general idea of governance. It necessarily involves institutions that cannot be completely free from the influence of social and political factors, for the simple reason governance is an organising concept for many areas covered by all social sciences. See Dixit (2009).

3. Inflation targetting has been the buzz expression in central banking circles for years till the recent global economic and financial crisis. It started with New Zealand adopting it as the sole objective of monetary policy in 1989. The main philosophy behind inflation targetting is that low and stable inflation would not only promote economic growth with its attendant reduction in the unemployment rate to its natural rate but also financial stability. The New Zealand example soon caught on and inflation targetting has been adopted subsequently in number of countries, including the UK, Sweden, Norway to name a few among the IEs either through legislation or through memoranda of understanding with the Treasuries. Such a memorandum exists in the case of the UK, to cite an example. The literature on inflation targetting is vast. One may however refer to the numerous writings of Lars Svensson and Frederic Mishkin. See for quick reading, Svensson (1999) (2005) (2010) and Mishkin (2000) (2002), Bernanke and Mishkin (1997). An excellent discussion on the growing limitation of inflation targetting as an approach to monetary policy pursuit took place at the First International Research Conference of the Reserve Bank of India in February 2010. See in particular the Transcript of the Governors' Panel Discussion on International Monetary System. See the website of the Reserve Bank of India, *http://www.rbi.org.in* Also see Subba Rao (2011).

2

The Institutional Requirements for Monetary Governance

Monetary governance requires that appropriate institutions and institutional mechanisms are established for formulating policies as well as for implementing the policies that are laid down by the authorities. While the institutions could be informally established or legally set up, it is important that fiscal and monetary authorities also have institutions for coordinating their policy actions as well for pursuing the objectives of macroeconomic policies. The institutional mechanisms required for coordination need to be workable and credible.

Institutional Setting for Policy Formulation

The institutional setting for sound monetary governance cannot be laid down as universally applicable. But in most countries, this is considered to be well set through the institution of committees or councils or groups. In many countries, committees/groups consist of membership drawn from outside the organisations/government entities. Some of the members are uber-confident economic modellers or pure academics or market players, besides technocrats with knowledge and experience of development administration, international economic dynamics and domestic economic and political market realities. External members are believed to be co-opted into the groups or committees on the basis of certain chosen criteria. The committee/group approach is expected to enable policies to be formulated with inputs from both external members and members from within, in economies where centralised decision-making is not the norm.

In general, most countries have committees for budget formulation and the financial policy of the government as well as for monetary policy. The budget formulation is normally very broad-based as well as process-based in that there will be inputs from all the Ministries and sometimes from the central banks as well. In most countries, the budget formulation exercise also involves consultations with those associated with business and trade and academics and analysts on the fiscal stance and specific tax or expenditure measures consistent with the overall financial policy. This process helps the fiscal authorities to work out the final budget for presentation to the legislators for their general consent. And the authorities make sure that secrecy in the final preparation of the budget is maintained for safeguarding the fiscal strength of the government as well as the stability of financial markets. Of course, that hardly prevents bloggers and analysts from providing their own views and speculating about the fiscal stance on the basis of the available macro indicators and about the possible measures that the governments are inclined to undertake. Such writings including the blogs often referred to as market expectations, while being triggered by the process relating to budget formulation and by the latest available information on macro indicators, could in the ultimate analysis, influence the final fiscal policy stance.

In all the governments in both industrial and emerging countries, there are, in addition, special advisory units/bodies/councils with economists at the top or near-top of them to advise the government of the measures to be taken for better economic policy formulation.[1] The membership positions in these bodies could be equivalent of the rank of cabinet minister. In some countries the governor or the deputy governor of the central bank would be part of such a setup either as full-fledged members or as special invitees. The policy formulation will focus not only on the development of the real sector but also on matters that pertain to the financial sector as well. The objectives of such institutional bodies are to ensure that growth, price stability and improved income and wealth distribution and promotion of human development and infrastructure growth would take place in a manner that trade-offs among them are optimal and in accordance with some desired/projected targets/trajectories for the year ahead. Such projections are made consistent with the medium-term trajectories. The periodic reports of these institutions are at times supplemented by technical papers. In some cases, such reports are placed on the websites or are published. In most cases, statements are released after meetings of the government economic advisory bodies.

Surprisingly enough, from the point of view of monetary governance, it is the institutional mechanism for formulating monetary policy that seems to fire the imagination of most analysts and the general public. This is so despite the fact that monetary policy making in many countries is not wholly concentrated in the top managements of central banks. Governments tend to be part of the monetary policy formulation groups or committees either as full-fledged members or special invitees with no voting rights. Governments' views apart, market functioning in the context of market integration and financial globalisation has seen to it that monetary policymakers provide an inkling of how the decisions are arrived at. This is considered as critical for good expectations formation, which feeds back as input into what is referred to as 'forward-looking' monetary policymaking, as if monetary policy unlike other economic policy areas is the only one with the forward look.

There are several models of institutions for monetary policymaking, of which one is the centralised one with decision-making concentrated in the central bank and fiscal authorities or in the Government-dominated central bank. Countries may choose to stylise such a centralised institutional structure as monetary policy committee but it is a euphemism since the membership structure consists of officials from the central bank and the government. The case in point is China. Variants of the centralised model can also be seen for example in the US among the IEs, Brazil and India among the emerging countries and surprisingly in some of the hard-core inflation targetting countries such as Canada, Chile and New Zealand as well.

In the US, traditionally, the Federal Open Market Committee (FOMC) announces key policy decisions relating to interest rate and the growth of money supply after deliberations among the members drawn from the Federal Reserve Board (FRB) and 12 Federal Reserve banks. The total membership of the committee, however, is restricted to 12 with voting rights. The chairman and the members of the FRB would be seven in number thus giving the advantage of the majority. Five members are drawn from the Federal Reserve banks of which one has to be the president of the Federal Reserve Bank of New York. The remaining four are drawn from the four groups of the Federal banks and are appointed for one-year terms on rotating basis. There is no external membership in the committee. However, all the Federal Reserve Bank presidents attend the meetings of the FOMC. The non-voting members are also allowed to discuss issues. The decision-making is generally consensus-driven.

In the European Central Bank (ECB), all monetary policy decisions are taken by the Governing Council consisting of governors of the Euro area National Central Banks (NCBs) and six members of the executive board of the ECB. Only 15 governors have voting rights and as of mid-2011 there are 17 governors but the voting membership is rotational. The ECB represents a nuanced variation of the US model, though the ECB believes that it has a combination of centralised and decentralised decision-making process.

In several other countries, monetary policy committees (MPCs) have representations from outside the central bank. Some of the committees have academics as full-fledged members. In the UK, the representative of the Government would be present but would have no voting right. In the case of an emerging country like India, the institutional setup in place is highly unusual. It has a Technical Advisory Committee consisting of the governor, deputy governors, a member or two of the Central Board of Directors, and outsiders (generally not more than five) that include academics and past central bankers and retired government officials. Their advice, however, would not be binding on the governor.

In Africa, a number of countries have in recent years formed MPCs. The ones with MPCs, to cite a few instances, are South Africa, Ghana and Nigeria. They have in general followed the convention of having officials as well as outsiders as members of the MPC with equal voting rights.

Countries with MPCs generally tend to provide to the wider public the voting patterns of members on the issues on the table and to publish the minutes of the meetings with some time lag. All central banks, irrespective of their model of decision-making process, release statements or communiques about the considerations that underlie their policy stance and measures.

It is difficult to know which type of institutional mechanism would best suit a country. There are no definitive criteria for making an informed choice among the available models of institutional mechanisms. Nevertheless, there is a general view among economists that a collegial or a committee oriented mechanism would be better than centralised mechanisms which could be biased depending on the personalities at the helm of affairs.[2] The argument in favour of committees, however, is not as robust as one imagines since there is recognition among bureaucrats in emerging economies, particularly those under democratic political structure, that it is best to have consultations with different stakeholders before taking a decision in order to gain credibility, and not necessarily go by the committee views which often tend to be consensual. A more important argument against the collegial or committee structure is that membership in the committee may consist of a majority of persons whose views are likely to be broadly in line with the leads that the authority gives about its policy preference through speeches and media interviews before the dates of the committee meetings. This would imply that the possibility of collusion or quasi-collusion among the committee members cannot be ruled out. Nonetheless, the decentralised institutional mechanism is increasingly favoured on the ground that it is possible to have built-in checks to possible collusion by rotating the membership in the committee every alternate year.

The advocacy for decentralised or a largely decentralised institutional mechanism is based on the ground that while central bank governors and deputy governors are appointees of the Government, it is essential that central banks are independent or at least autonomous of the Ministries of Finance for formulating credible policies.[3] The advocacy for independence is not so much on matters relating to personnel management and financial budget management as on issues relating to policy pursuit. The theoretical basis for this argument lies in the doctrine of the time inconsistency.[4] A policy would be time consistent, so the explanation goes, if a policy action proposed to be taken in time t for time t+1 remains optimal for implementation when t+1 actually materialises. In other words, as Walsh (1998) has argued, the new economic information that becomes available between the period t and t+1 would not make a difference to the optimality of the policy action that will be taken in period t+1.[5] The public has to believe that the central bank is committed to controlling prices. To this economists add that central banks should not be led by considerations of increasing the level of output or employment by using credit/money supply mechanism to augment aggregate demand.

The above argument rests on the strong belief that it would be best to enable central banks to eschew inflation bias in their actions with a fixed policy rule such as a firm commitment to a specific order of inflation. Rogoff (1985) in fact suggested that the governors of central banks should be persons with such commitment to inflation control.[6] However, central banks, faced with enormous economic uncertainties, would not be able to specify the order of inflation that is planned to be achieved in t+1 period. In such a case, there has to be a feedback rule to allow central bank to respond to shocks in an orderly manner.

The argument that central banks have inherent inflation bias has not however been empirically proved. This is not to say that the bias cannot be induced by governments in countries where central banks have no degree of autonomy. Such instances leading to high four-digit inflations are well known in recent history. Latin America and East European countries for instance have witnessed such bizarre inflationary conditions in the 20th century.[7] In these instances, central banks have been lax in respect of money supply creation, partly under pressure of governments in power. In the event, it is difficult to generalise that the inaction is sufficient evidence of inflation bias of central banks. Central banks have been created essentially to eliminate the misuse by governments in creating money at will. The very rationale of the existence of central banks thus is essentially based on the idea that money should be valued in a precise way because excess of it can lead to high price increases. Equally true is that modern day governments that are very mindful of the need to keep inflation under control are as much anti-inflation protagonists as central banks. It must be recognised that there are many instances when governments in power were defeated in elections when inflation rates soared beyond the public's margin of tolerance.[8]

Institutional Setting for Policy Implementation

The institutional mechanisms for implementation of policies and the processes that they entail would generally be internally driven with enunciation of the guiding principles for the conduct of the participants within the organisation or entity (including the ministry). The institutional mechanism in the organisation/entity could be single or in the form of a number of committees or groups with or without any representation from outside sources. In many emerging economies, in the governments, the bureaucracy lays down the rules and practices consistent with the law of the land. Whether the rules are complied with or not is a question that is supposedly addressed periodically through evaluation reports or impact studies for internal guidance and in most cases for complying with the requirements of the parliamentary committees or tribunals. Incentives for proper and expeditious implementation are often grafted into the rules for conduct of the staff.

There could be any number of committees or groups to deal with governance relating to taxation, expenditures and debt, both domestic and external. What they focus is on compliance to the rules by officials, for it is as important as the compliance to the law by tax-paying individuals and firms and by contract enforcing agencies. In regard to debt, however, the cost and timing of the debt issues would have to be internally laid down with due consultations with stake-holders including central banks and with clear recognition of the market conditions. In general, compliance would be high if the cost of non-compliance is made prohibitively high. This is particularly important if one were to reduce the spread of corruption in public life.

In most central banks, there are departments that deal with financial markets. The department's overall work and its activity would again be guided by committees or groups that are formally or informally set up by central banks for closely monitoring market conditions on a daily basis in order to determine the required liquidity in the system that would be consistent with the demand for liquidity. There will be no outside members in such committees or groups.

Ideally such committees or groups should meet 'daily'. It should be small-sized consisting of senior executives of the departments dealing with monetary policy, financial markets and research. The daily meetings should be presided over by the deputy governor in charge of monetary policy and research or operations or in her/his absence, the executive director in charge of monetary policy or operations. The meetings should be of short duration of, say 30 minutes and could be held once or twice depending on the market conditions. They could be informal without any formal notes. They should result in one-line or two-line recommendation to the governor about the actions that may be considered for the day in any of the markets (money market or foreign exchange market) under the central bank's jurisdiction (this could include no action) along with the main reasoning behind the recommendations.

It is possible that governors may not always be available for giving their guidance to such committees or groups at the headquarters of the central banks. In such cases, the deputy governor in charge of the central bank should take the decision marking at the same time, the recommendation of the committee or group to the governor for his/her subsequent notice. In general, there should be a formal administrative rule that at least one deputy governor or executive director should be always available at the corporate office of the central bank for purposes of effective governance of central banks on all days.

The decisions of the implementation committees/groups in central banks are expected to be implemented immediately by the concerned officials. Problems, however, arise when implementation committees are not supported by mechanisms that are capable of implementation. This would be the case if the rules and processes are either not clearly laid down or not properly understood by all those who are entrusted with the task of acting on the decisions of the implementation committees. The latter is often the case. The personnel handling the operations should be therefore trained and their responsibilities and limits should be clearly defined and monitored regularly. Rules for staff conduct in central banks have clauses for compliance and they should be applied without any forbearance.

Institutional Mechanisms for Coordination of Actions of Macroeconomic Policymakers

The architecture of monetary governance should be such as to ensure coordination of actions of governments and central banks for the sake of consistency in the pursuit of macroeconomic policy and for elimination of perceptions of policy uncertainty among the market participants. In most countries, there are mechanisms for policy coordination that may or may not be formally constituted. Such policy coordination groups are often headed by the minister or a very high-ranked official of the government. Coordination is also implied in the way the monetary policymaking committees are constituted and the considerations that such committees should keep in view.[9]

The setup for such policy coordination is not the same as the one that is needed for a separate setup for coordinating the actions of all financial regulators including the Government. The institutional coordination committees are generally but not always headed by central banks in some EMEs.

The two separate institutional arrangements for coordination, one for macro policy and the other for regulatory oversight, would be important given the need for closer monitoring of the financial markets for ensuring banking and financial stability. Central banks could be in charge of the regulatory oversight committees, without implying that governments have no stake in banking and financial stability. But where central banks are in charge of the regulatory committees, it is necessary that central banks hold consultations with the government at appropriate time since regulatory reforms form part of the overall economic reforms. There could also be situations when the heads of governments (Prime Ministers or Presidents) or Finance Ministers could convene a joint meeting of the two coordination groups for discussion on matters that affect all the three major objectives of growth, price stability and financial stability. This has in fact happened in both IEs and EMEs during the recent financial crisis.

One of the challenges to monetary governance is in regard to the autonomy as well as the seniority that should be given to the institutional arrangements for coordination of regulatory bodies including the central bank. There is in general no one universally accepted view among the academics as well as policy analysts on the matter. It has to be therefore country-specific. Where the financial sector is largely or dominantly owned by the governments, the financial sector coordination groups tend to be headed by the governments rather than the central banks as is presently the case in India. In such situations, the vice-chairperson would be the central bank governor. This does not mean that central banks do not have any influence on the overarching issues of financial governance. For instance, financial stability reports are still brought out by central banks and not by governments every year, generally twice. These reports are known to influence public opinion and pressurise the chairpersons to act in line with the market realities and long-term perspectives of financial development.

There was until recently a highly rated model of a separate organisational structure to look into all aspects of coordination of supervision and regulation of the entire financial sector as had been the case in the UK. This model came under heavy criticism during the recent financial crisis since it hardly helped to detect the symptoms of the crisis that enveloped the financial markets in recent years. The failure of the Financial Supervisory Authority (FSA) in the UK is an example of the failed financial governance essentially because it ignored the need for integrating macro-policy considerations with supervision, so vital for promoting effectiveness of financial regulation.

The International Face of Monetary Governance: Brief Sketch

A nation's monetary governance will necessarily have international dimension, since policy actions of a country could impact other countries' economic performance by virtue of integration of real and financial activities across countries, an aspect on which we shall deal in some detail in Chapter 5. To be brief here, global monetary governance has become relevant in view of the growing integration of economies. But as it is difficult for each nation to monitor issues of global monetary governance on a daily basis, nations surrender that task to 'representative' executive boards within the international organisations themselves. However, the influence of a nation on the executive boards which act as proxies to global monetary governance would rest on its relative economic strength in the world economy. Unless the relative strength improves either individually or in partnership with a group of similarly placed countries, a chair in the executive board would not be able to hold a sufficiently strong lever of influence when decisions have to be taken in the ultimate analysis.[10]

The executive boards are at best proxies but the real economic power on the international scene is wielded by groups of countries such as the Group of Seven (G-7) or the Group of Twenty (G-20). G-7 seems to have lost much of its relevance in the last four years. The G-20, on the other hand, seems to be influencing the policy-impacting organs of the IMF and the WB, namely the International Monetary and Financial Committee (IMFC) and the Development Committee (DC) respectively as well as the Executive Board either explicitly or in a subtle fashion.

On their part, G-20 meetings are held every now and then and communiques are issued at the end of each of these meetings. The main issue is whether the decisions of the group are concretised into operational numbers and are implemented in good time by the international community of which the IMF and the WB are important parts and in a manner that promotes the international good. It is also important that as a group, the G-20 should revisit the representation within it. There are also no governance principles that are placed on the group. With regard to representation in the group, at present, Saudi Arabia represents the Middle East and South Africa represents Africa while the East Europe has no representation. These regions have a fairly large population. A number of countries in these regions as well as in the highly populated Asia are likely to demand representation in the group by virtue of their growing economic performance. This is a challenge that the international community will have to face in not too distant a future.

The IMF and the WB, on their part, will have to lay down the best principles of governance mechanisms for their own internal working in the present context of the fixed number of chairs with some of them representing a large number of countries.[11] Besides, the governance mechanisms should focus also on those areas where member countries' coordination efforts are needed for improved functioning of the international economic and financial system. In this regard, the initiatives that have so far been taken by the IMF and the WB have been largely at the behest of IEs, in particular the US.

This is attributable to the fact that there are very few EMEs where dedicated teams of researchers of international relations are formed in governments and central banks and their policy notes periodically discussed by those who regularly represent their governments at the meetings of the G-20 or the G-20 sub-groups or technical groups. There are also no instances of sanctions, not even verbal, on countries that have triggered problems in the functioning of the international financial system and that have not complied with the recommendations, open or implied that the IMF/WB staff members make during their Article IV consultations or country missions. This failure reflects in part the high quota strength of IEs and the attendant voting strength.

Matters relating to quotas and quota formulas as well as the voting requirements will continue to be dominant for years to come despite some recognition in the IEs of the growing economic strength of some of the emerging countries of the world in recent years. This is seen in the fact that the shares of a few emerging economies have improved in the latest quota dispensation. However, as the IMF publications (2008) and (2010 a and 2010b) show, there is very little shift in the balance of governance of the international institutions from the traditionally classified IEs to the group of emerging and developing countries.[12]

End Notes

1. In the US, the Council of Economic Advisers attached to the president wields considerable influence on the economic policies pursued by the administration in power. In emerging economies too such institutional mechanisms exist. For example, in India, the Prime Minister's Economic Advisory Council performs a similar function though its influence on the economic policies seems to be not as much felt as in the US.
2. Committees are said to help make better decisions than individuals, according to the literature which is vast. Surveys of the literature by Blinder (2007b), Bergr *et al.* (2008), Fujiki (2005), Gerling *et al.* (2005), may be seen in this connection. However, there is no agreement among economists on how large a committee should be, though the opinion seems to veer round somewhat small-sized committees of 5-9 members.

3. The literature on central bank independence is very vast and has been very widely discussed since almost the middle of 1980s. For a good basic summary of the positions of economists and for a general evaluation of the issue of central bank independence and autonomy, see the relevant chapter in Vasudevan (2003).
4. The most cited article is that of Kydland and Prescott (1977). Later an equally important article on the subject by Barro and Gordon (1983) appeared but it has not been as much cited as that of Kydland and Prescott.
5. This would be a plausible argument if the gap between the periods, t and t+1 is short. If the time gap is large, the latest economic information could make a difference to the initially agreed optimality position as the recent financial crisis experience has shown.
6. Rogoff's argument in retrospect appears somewhat odd since it is difficult to believe that central bank governors by nature and by training are inflation-biased, a point that is being discussed later in this chapter. This is not to say that there cannot be differences in the degrees of commitment among central bankers to the general objective of inflation control. It is, however, possible that there are times when inflation does not pose a problem and promotion of employment and growth could be a major challenge. In such a situation, central banks may place a higher degree of emphasis on growth than they normally do.
7. The German inflation of 1923 often described as 'hyper' is well known, thanks to the seminal work of Bresciani Turroni (original English edition: 1937). In the 1980s, Argentina, Bolivia, Brazil, Mexico and Israel have experienced very high inflation, with some of them recording more than 1,000 per cent a year. Argentina had over 4,000 per cent annualised inflation rate in 1989, Bolivia as much as 8,175 per cent in 1985, Brazil over 1,100 per cent in 1992 and Mexico about 159 per cent in 1987. Israel had annualised inflation rate of 445 per cent in 1984.
8. There are many instances of governments losing power owing to the prevalence of high inflation even in emerging economies as for example India.
9. In so far as institutional mechanism for policy coordination is concerned, it is the Finance Ministry or the Treasury which exercises a right to be the main coordinator of macroeconomic policy by virtue of the fact that governments are elected and are required to pursue all the objectives of economic policy. Even where the central banks are considered to be autonomous, the objectives of their monetary policy committees are not always in support of price stability as the only objective to be pursued. There is an erroneous view that central banks that are mandated to pursue the objective of price stability are totally autonomous and can take policy measures that are inconsistent with the economic policy of the government. The UK's position clearly clarifies this issue in that its policy actions would have to be supportive of the government's overall economic policy. This is also the case with a frontier market economy such as Nigeria which has inserted this idea in Section 12 of the Central Bank of Nigeria Act, 2007. The Section states under sub-section (1): In order to *facilitate* the attainment of the objective of price stability and to *support* the economic policy of the Federal Government, there shall be a Committee of the Bank known as the Monetary Policy Committee (italics added by the author).
10. This becomes evident during the discussions on quota increases in the IMF for emerging and developing countries. The discussions in 2010 at the executive

board suggest that in general there has not been a radical departure from the formulas that underlie quota calculations over the last 50 years or so. Similarly, the discussions about the heads of the IMF and the WB have also been dominated by countries or groups of countries that have most quota/voting strength in the executive boards. This privileged position may not be easily given up in the near future despite remonstrations to the contrary by individual countries among the IEs or by the IEs as a group.

11. The executive boards in the IMF and the WB have a fixed number of chairs. Some chairs are represented by a group of countries and some chairs are represented by single member nations. The US and the UK, for example, always held the chairs representing their countries. The US has more than 15 per cent voting power and can veto a number of critical issues by virtue of the fact that in respect of certain policy issues or organisational issues, 85 per cent majority of the votes cast would be required as per the Articles of Agreement. Majority of chairs represent a number of nations. Countries have a choice in joining a chair even if they are not contiguously linked in geographical sense with the main country holding the chair. In the case of some chairs, the position of the executive director rotates. The entire continent of Africa, numbering 54 countries, is represented by only two chairs. The executive directors are expected to represent their governments' views and make interventions relating to their own countries and policy issues. They could, if they like, make their views known on the issues arising from the surveillance reports on other member states.

12. China was in particular the main beneficiary of the most recent quota dispensation. However, it is worth noting that despite being the second largest economy in the world and a major contributor to global growth, it has been given third place in the quota shares in the IMF. India, yet another emerging country with the second highest contribution to global growth occupies the eighth position in the overall IMF quota share. IEs as a group retain 57.7 per cent of the total quotas with the remaining portion being provided for emerging and developing countries. The US still retains the veto power on crucial issues such as the quota dispensation. The so-called 2008 IMF reform has meant that IEs have lost only 2.8 percentage point from their share of 60.5 per cent. The relative strength of countries mentioned here is measured on the PPP-based calculation of gross national product of countries.

3

The Rainbow of Interests

Monetary governance has to be concerned not merely with the institutional requirements but also with the management of the rainbow of interests of the principal actors (namely the government and the central bank) and the stakeholders (as for example, commercial banks, insurance companies, pension fund management entities, foreign exchange dealers and operators, equity and hedge funds, mutual funds and other brokers, dealers and forward transaction contractors) that interact with them. The principal actors are led by public policymaking for the good of the society while a large number of other stakeholders are generally oriented towards maximising profits or returns.

The Principal Actors

Merging or uniting the interests of the principal actors is critical and will have to have two elements which, however, are not mutually exclusive. First, there has to be a clear demarcation of one's own activity-jurisdictions. Secondly, the relationship between them should not smack of the principal-agent framework wherein the Ministry of Finance assumes the role of the principal and the central bank is placed in the role of its agent.[1] The first element is legally given. It is well known and could be operated in a flexible manner to reflect the changing world economic environment. It is the second element that can be tricky in terms of its resolution. For, it is well known that the principal-agent framework is often the case in many EMEs and to an extent in some IEs as well. The relationship, however, becomes complicated when the agent is as well informed as the principal. In such a situation, it is possible that the principal and the agent could be in game-theoretic mode, notwithstanding the open support for fostering incentives for realisation of some common objectives of growth and inflation control and for complying with the legal set of contracts. Playing games may not lead to coalescing of interests with the result the attainment of common good could become a distant reality.

Fiscal Authorities

The bandwidth of services that fiscal authorities provide is large. Our concern here is with the services that the fiscal authorities provide to the financial sector. This concern may need to be viewed in the context of the relationship of the government with the central bank or with the agents of the government (usually commercial banks) that are so designated by the central bank especially where central bank offices do not exist. Central banks are bankers to governments. Central banks maintain government balances in their books of account and facilitate payment and settlement systems relating to all government payments and government receipts. Besides, many central banks manage government debt although this function has been hived off from the central banks in recent years in some countries.[2] It is in relation to debt management that the interests of central banks and fiscal authorities could come into conflict when central banks set short-term interest rate and operate upon the instrument of open market operations to guide the interest rate movements that are inconsistent with the government's interest in selling bonds of different maturities at different coupon rates. It is said that this problem could be resolved by assigning the function of debt management to a separate entity. However, it is not yet proven that creation of a separate debt management office either outside the Finance Ministry or as its unit is the best way of managing public finances and of ensuring that the debt management objectives are met by governments that in fact could act inconsistently on grounds of changing economic circumstances.[3] It is also not clear whether retaining of the debt management function within the central bank with definitive rules and policy councils with the government official as its chairperson could be of help especially when public debt is high and public's confidence in the governments' ability to rein in fiscal deficits is eroded as had been the case in the wake of the debate on European and US debt crises during the period, April-October 2011.

There are also other areas where conflicts of interests could arise. For example, in some countries, fiscal authorities own some if not all domestic (as against foreign) commercial banks or own large shares in them.[4] In such cases, central banks as regulators may come in conflict with the functioning of the public sector banks especially when the financial intermediation services rendered by the public sector banks are found to be driven not so much by considerations of efficiency and stability of credit and other related financial markets as by the whims of the ministers or top officials of the government. There could be also situations where governments may force publicly owned banks to buy government bonds much beyond the reasonable limits set either conventionally in accordance with the principle of profit optimisation or by central bank directives.

Conflict of interests could arise also in other areas such as the ones where central banks are encouraged to act as advisers to the governments on economic and financial issues. The relationship between them could be rendered fragile when central banks take this function far too seriously and air their views openly without considering the perceptions that their views tend to often leave among the informed and often influential opinion-makers. In general, central banks are consulted by governments on certain issues of importance for both the authorities. Consultations imply that central banks would not air their views on the issues referred to them in the public. Even where issues such as the size of the fiscal deficit constrain flexibility in monetary management, central banks are not expected to articulate openly their opposition or disagreement to the size of the fiscal deficit. This would particularly be the case if in the budget formulation process the deficit figures that emerge are a product of consultations that include those with the central bank. The ways of financing of deficit matter most to central banks. For, the financing sources would provide clues to the governments about the extent of support that could be expected from the banking sector including the central bank and from other financial institutions. The consultation process also provides an idea to the central banks of the public sector's contribution to the aggregate demand stimulus. From the budget figures of deficit and the extent of support of the financial sector to the stated deficit, market analysts will be able to guess the positioning of the market rates of interest and the likely inclination of the yield curve.

Central banks, on their part, with the given information about the governments' budget, would be able to work out the extent of monetary stimulus that the economy would need that would be consistent with the anticipated supply position. Once the fiscal and external sector positions are reckoned in the calculus of money, the central bank will be able to explain the stance of monetary policy. Central banks surely would be able to indicate the fiscal impact on aggregate demand and on prices with greater definiteness than the effect that the external sector developments would leave on demand and prices.

Harmonisation of interests of fiscal and monetary authorities is essential for creating a climate of macroeconomic stability and policy certainty which are critical for other economic stakeholders so that consumer confidence and investment sentiment can be maintained at levels that would help attain growth close to potential level and realise inflation in line with the desired rate. After all, both the authorities are led by the same objective of promoting and implementing public policies for overall good of the society. Public good thus is the primordial objective which translates essentially into economic diversification and development of activities with due regard to ecology and environment, regulation for stability of both the real and financial sectors. From these two major objectives would flow a number of sub-objectives.

Central Banks

The services that central banks offer are several. Some of the prominent ones are: issuance of currency, provision of payment and settlement systems, banker to government and to banks, supervision (where applicable) and regulation of banks and other financial intermediaries, monetisation of debt where debt management is part of the central bank function and reserve management for promoting the best national interests. In all the areas of services, the public good and not profit-making will be the main motivating force. This objective does not mean that central banks do not reap profits or generate surpluses in the financial sense. After all, printing of currency and managing its circulation generate seigniorage by virtue of the fact that the face value of the currency note would be higher than its intrinsic value.[5] But the profits that central banks make in the process are in most cases transferred either wholly or to a substantial extent to the governments. A part of the profits is earmarked for creating reserves to meet unexpected circumstances such as fluctuations in the value of foreign exchange assets or government securities or other securities that central banks hold. There are also instances when central banks placed a portion of the profits into funds created specifically for fostering development of particular economic sectors such as agriculture or industry and/or for stabilising the fluctuations in output in agriculture. Such an approach was in fact followed in India in the past, at least till development banks took possession of the special funds created for the purpose in the Reserve Bank of India.[6]

It must, however, be acknowledged that the central focus of central banks is not profit-making but playing by the rules to promote an environment that would help realise public good to a significant extent. Currency issued is based on definitive rules of sound backing of foreign exchange assets, gold and government securities issued by a government that is not bankrupt and is considered as a credible borrower. Payment structure of central banks aims to ensure that settlements are done with certainty—a public good—within reasonable time and in amounts specified on the instruments in question. As part of improving efficiency, central banks encourage commercial banks in the payment system to have compatible technologies that could interface with the domestic as well as international payment technologies. To ensure that such compatible technological systems exist, payment and settlement systems are subject to codes and standards as well as surveillance and audit systems.[7] The function of being the banker to government could have rules relating to the extent to which the government could borrow against securities at a specified rate of interest with a discretion given to the central bank to lend beyond the limit as secured overdraft up to a certain proportion of the original loan limit at a rate of interest that would be higher than the one charged on the amounts borrowed by the government under the normal loan limit. Such lending rules, however, differ from country to country. But the essence of having such rules is to ensure that fiscal discipline prevails and aggregate demand kept under check. Aggregate demand flare-up, fuelled by excessive fiscal expenditures, leads to price increases or price instability. To heighten the essence of public good, some emerging economies have either placed rules on government borrowings and on overdraft positions as part of legal commitments or under memoranda of understanding.[8]

In some countries, the central banks, apart from managing public debt, lay down guidelines about external commercial borrowings of public sector commercial enterprises as well as private sector entities in close collaboration with the government. As of now, this is the case in India. But it is often pointed out that central banks as regulators of banking industry should not be managers of public debt which is often held by the banking industry essentially because of the central banks' regulations relating to liquidity ratios.[9] This is considered as an area where there will emerge the problem of conflict of interest. This is one of the major reasons why in a number of industrialised and emerging countries, the debt management function has been shifted to a separate entity. However, this does not necessarily imply that the debt management entities are entirely autonomous and are outside the influence of the fiscal authorities or as a matter of fact even the monetary authorities.[10] It is possible to point out that since public debt requirements are worked out with reference to the final objectives of growth and price stability, it is necessary to have an institutional mechanism that would coordinate the viewpoints of the Finance Ministry and central bank irrespective of the fact that debt management operations are located in an organisational sense, outside the fiscal or monetary authorities. In other words, it is not as important to have debt management entrusted to a separate entity as to have a coordinating mechanism that in any case exists in an informal manner in most countries. The only reason that one could adduce in favour of having a separate debt management entity is that it would help bring in transparency in the operations in the government's dependence on resources outside the regular sources of revenue.

Central banks acting as bankers to commercial banks are led again by the consideration of public good. The rules relating to this function could be several. But in all countries, central banks have been traditionally extending very short-term loans (often overnight) to commercial banks against specified collaterals that are not subject to any volatility in their values at pre-determined interest rates. The traditional approach of the central banks is often viewed as an extension of the argument that every central bank should be a lender of the last resort, a' la Walter Bagehot (1873). During the recent financial crisis, however, the lender of the last resort function has been further extended and loan facilities at the central banks were relaxed in both industrialised and emerging economies. For example, in the US, the Fed provided in addition to the traditional collateralised short-term loan facility, several other facilities. They are: 'term asset-backed securities loan facility' to banks along with term deposit facility, 'MM investor funding facility', 'ABCP MMMF liquidity facility', 'CP funding facility', 'primary dealer credit facility', 'term securities lending facility' and 'term auction facility'. Provision of these facilities was defended on the ground that they help ensure that key credit markets have adequate liquidity to meet the perceived high demand for credit. Such an action, however, implies a correct choice of collateral (not necessarily in line with the real bills doctrine) and that it will not trigger inflation expectations. But these considerations were hardly evident in the actions of the central banks in many IEs. A new expression was coined to defend the Fed's extraordinary and unusual approach to its lending. The expression 'quantitative easing' or 'credit easing' came into the lexicon of central banking.[11] The general view is that had these extraordinary measures been not taken, there could be a prolongation of recessionary conditions and continuation of the strains on banking and financial stability. The actions of central banks that eased credit helped to bolster their balance sheets. They were considered to have promoted financial stability as public good.

It is, however, important to recognise that financial stability concerns cannot be addressed by mere quantitative splurge of central bank credit. They require to be also addressed by revisiting the supervisory and regulatory structure and ring-fence the financial system with tighter norms and regulations. Fortunately, this was acknowledged by the IEs and the international financial community in general. In the result, the Basle norms have been tightened and moves towards Basle III had been initiated.[12] Besides, the functioning of a number of financial markets and financial instruments had come under closer scrutiny.[13] However, whenever a new financial market is fostered or a financial instrument is introduced, it is necessary for the national authorities to exercise due diligence while granting permissions to operate in the national boundaries. Such initiatives by national authorities will have to be forward looking in the sense that as financial markets develop, there will be pressures to open up new markets and new instruments. Acquiescence to such pressures should be preceded by actions to lay down ground rules of regulation in the proposed areas of activity and to devise the machinery and technical capacities required to monitor and implement such rules.

The accommodative policy of governments through larger public spending and central banks could not have taken place in 2009 and to a large extent in 2010 without the central banks compromising the quality of assets for lending and the fiduciary rules relating to the backing of assets for currency issue and lowering the policy rates of interest. In IEs, 'quantitative easing' (QE) or 'credit easing' (CE) was accompanied by monetary policy rates being brought down to zero or near zero. The quantitative easing (QE) or credit easing (CE) approach has stemmed further deterioration in the financial position of banks and other financial institutions but it had signalled tolerance for unsound monetary governance.

The QE/CE approach was supposed to take care not merely of the objective of promoting financial stability but also of the objective of turning around the economy to growth path. It was assumed implicitly that growth would be reflected in pick up in a sharp reduction in the unemployment rate. It was also believed that once the economy rebounds, the accommodative policy could be reversed to bring the economy back to *status quo ante*. However, at least till the second quarter of 2011 there has been no substantive evidence of a definitive sustainable recovery in industrialised countries. In fact, the unemployment rate has been hovering at over 9 per cent in the United States as at mid-2011. As at mid-2011, the debt to GDP ratio has also been high at over 95 per cent raising doubts about fiscal sustainability of the US. In the UK, the unemployment rate is placed at 8 per cent in mid-2011, with debt to GDP ratio at little over 80 per cent. The countries in Euro area have debt to GDP ratios that average about 85 per cent, with Greece, Italy, Belgium and Ireland in the lead with over or near 100 per cent. Growth rates in many countries were in negative zone and those that recorded positive rates were nowhere near the rates posted in the years before the global economic and financial crisis.

The QE/CE method however was not followed by all the countries for economic recovery purposes. The dilemma as to whether QE/CE method should be followed was present in many EMEs. Their problem was not about recovering from recessionary conditions for they had posted high growth rates even before 2008. But in view of global integration, they recognised the need to address any possible shortfall in external demand for their exports that could lead to output deceleration. Hence, both the governments and central banks resorted to expansionary policies without following the QE/CE method of easing. For, in some EMEs, central bank money or base money or reserve money had increased even prior to the global financial crisis owing to large capital inflows.[14] And in some EMEs, recovery from the global financial crisis began fairly quickly after a short period of fiscal and monetary expansion that helped boost domestic demand to offset the shortfall in external demand. The pick-up in domestic demand contributed to improvement in growth though the surge in excess demand that occurred as a result had pulled up prices. The exit from accommodative policy in EMEs meant that not only fiscal discipline has to be set in place but also monetary policies have to be tightened with policy rate hikes and in some cases, increases in cash reserve ratios (CRRs). Although the increases in CRR contributed to the increase in base money, the balance sheets of most EMEs did not increase as significantly as in IEs.

Central banks' concern for preserving growth for public good may need to be seen in yet another context. The high capital flows into EMEs in recent years had led to monetary expansion and currency appreciation. Monetary governance required that the countries ensure that stability in domestic credit growth is maintained and volatility in capital flows be reduced. It is in this context, some EMEs have imposed or tightened capital controls so as to insure themselves from any adverse impact of 'sudden stops',[15] with central banks and governments acting in concert, again bringing about a rainbow of interests for the public good.

The Principal Actors and Other Stakeholders: Interface

The interests of other stakeholders (other than regulators of securities, insurance and pension funds) arise essentially from their pursuit of the objective of profit maximisation. However, fiscal and monetary authorities along with relevant official regulators regulate the activities of 'other' stakeholders for public good. It is taken for granted that the interface hinges only on regulation by the authorities. Regulation is only one side of the overall picture. There is also a need for leveraging market discipline. Market discipline and effective regulation have to go hand in hand. Market discipline, is not to be taken as given with the hope that the legislative enactments covering different markets—banking, insurance, securities, pension and other intermediaries would ensure market discipline.

Market Discipline

Why is it that ensuring effective market discipline is not easy? Is there a problem of failure of not constructing an appropriate synthesis of interests of the regulators and other stakeholders? Perhaps so. First there is the question of information about the market—the total volume, the rates of transactions, the number of players and the transparency in the signing in and settlement of transactions. Information cannot be collected without incurring costs. At times, they are provided at high costs and may still not be readily available to all those who seek information including the active market participants. There exists information asymmetry in the markets in many economies, both in the industrialised and emerging world, whether one likes or not.[16] Clearly defining transparency practices for both public and private corporate entities as part of corporate governance would be essential to alleviate the cost of information asymmetry. Secondly, sound incentives are needed for market discipline to thrive. Incentives are essential so that regulation does not become very burdensome to implement and costly. It is here the operational part of the regulatory framework has to show some foresight in recognising market and non-market incentives and build them into the very structure of the framework. Such recognition and the consequential actions are rarely seen in many countries, in particular developing and emerging economies. Even where such incentives seem to exist at least on paper, there are voices of scepticism.

The sceptics, at least many of them, often believe that self-regulation would be the best approach to adopt. Self-regulation, however, is not an alternative. It could at best be complementary to the regulatory framework that has inherent incentive structure. Such a blended approach is critical to address the risks of cross-sector exposures and cross-country exposures that have been the characteristic of the recent financial crisis. One might argue that exposure risks can be taken care of by resorting to hedging mechanisms but a priori it is often difficult to know how good the available hedging mechanisms would be. Transparency and timely and accurate disclosure are needed to assess the types and locations of risks and to distinguish the financial firms by their financial strength and asset exposures. Finally, market discipline hinges on the degree of effectiveness of the corporate governance mechanisms in all the financial institutions—a task that is never easy to accomplish.

Regulations and Regulatory Structure

Theoretically, it is possible to construct a rainbow of interests with sound regulations and with appropriate mechanisms for monitoring and screening all on paper. But one should recognise that they cannot be laid down as universally applicable best practices—a fact that is not being fully absorbed in the circles that produce international standards.[17] They have to be tuned to the market and institutional realities of the countries in question. In India, both fiscal and monetary authorities together worked out standards and codes suitable to the country's needs and adopted supervision standards even though its central bank did not face the financial crisis of the order that the US and the UK faced in 2008 and 2009 partly due to its distinct codes and well functional operational apparatus. Some analysts however felt that India escaped the crisis not because of institutional setup or its implementation of its own standards but because of capital controls. This argument also said to be valid in the case of China, has some merit but if capital controls alone could work as a buffer, then one may ask as to how Canada with no capital controls could escape the financial crisis. Canada among the IEs is uniquely distinct in that it did not face the financial crisis of the kind that the US, the UK and other IEs have faced mainly because of its carefully tuned up supervisory and regulatory structure that ensured market compliance and discipline. This is what sound regulation would ultimately mean. It would also mean that the general tendency of many an emerging country to blindly follow the regulatory framework as found in the US, the UK and in the Euro zone would not necessarily be good to the countries even if they get nods of approval of their actions from the World Bank and the IMF and their not so distant cousin, the BIS.

The Concerns to be Still Addressed

In the recent episode of the financial crisis, the main aim of most IEs, however, was to ensure that their financial institutions did not collapse. This was their immediate aim. However, they had to also relax regulations on the financial institutions for some defined periods of time in order to avoid the costs of rigid application of regulations in an environment of global economic uncertainty. These actions, however, are not the same as bailouts that were initially undertaken in the US and the UK. The public resentment over the actions of the US and the UK governments to bail out financial institutions led the authorities to turn to forbearance, a principle which was not allowed under the original framework of international standards and codes. The forbearance entailed costs but it was thought that it will be limited to a short-term period.[18] Besides, the very structures for supervision came under scrutiny. For example, the FSA which was once hailed as the ideal mechanism to bring about coordinated set of actions has failed to deliver, forcing the UK to revisit the model and think of a policy board that would be under the jurisdiction of the authorities that are charged with monetary governance as we have defined here. Besides, the discussions on the existing Basle norms and on strengthening them over the medium term focussed on the idea of augmenting and regulating capital, along with stringent provisioning consistent with periods of economic cycles.

There are still many other concerns despite the recent initiatives at establishing relatively sound supervisory and regulatory regimes in many countries.

First, sound supervision and regulation would help cushion the economy of financial shocks but it would not facilitate economic growth unless regulations are such that the financial system helps provide services that promote growth. But more empirical studies are required for gaining insights on regulation-growth relationship.[19] Secondly, it is still not clear as to what has prevented the authorities to investigate as to why the regulations in place were not complied with and why accountability for non-compliance was not appropriately and quickly applied. Thirdly, no view has yet emerged as to whether financial institutions that are in severe financial stress should be bailed out or provided with the fence of forbearance without any conditions and without regard to the costs and burdens on the society at large. The severity of this problem had become glaring in the initial instance mainly because of the blind acceptance of the 'too big to fail' argument in the case of large financial institutions.[20] One may also need to ask whether bailouts and forbearance should be more than temporary. Finally, financial innovations, as for example, credit default swaps (CDS)[21] and collateralised debt obligations (CDOs)[22] which seemed to have allowed regulations to be circumvented and facilitated executives to earn large bonuses may not necessarily be able to improve financial sector development. All financial innovative products need to be screened and monitored by fiscal and/or monetary authorities under the umbrella of financial regulation and with a view to ensuring that the operations of the products do not jeopardise growth impulses.

End Notes

1. For simple elucidation of the principal-agent problem, see Stiglitz (1987). The formulation of the problem rests on the idea that where one actor (the principal) has an incentive to delegate power to another actor (the agent) with an expectation that the agent will, on obtaining the powers delegated to him/her, act in such a manner that would be in consonance with the initial expectations or preferences of the principal. The delegation of power is often led by the consideration of reducing transaction costs. Transaction costs arise mainly due to information asymmetries. Information asymmetries are associated with the issues of adverse selection and moral hazard. Adverse selection occurs when a person in power does not know the best candidate for the job and may therefore appoint a person whose price is quoted higher than his/her economic worth. In the case of the banking industry, the banker makes a selection of the borrowers

not merely on the value of the collaterals offered close to the banker's initial expectation but also on the basis of what the borrowers are willingness to pay as higher interest rates. Moral hazard arises when the employer does not know the person who is employed. In the case of the banking industry, it will mean that the borrower in question would not be known to the banker well enough before the time of the selection of the borrower. The problem of moral hazard, however, could be avoided if the employer/banker designs a contract that offers enough incentive to function efficiently. Also see articles on the subject by Grossman (1983), Harris and Raviv (1979) and Chortareas and Miller (2002).

2. Public debt management essentially aims at fulfilling government's financing needs through borrowing from public (including financial and non-financial institutions) at the lowest possible cost over the medium to long term. It is also expected that public debt management is undertaken with prudent degree of risk. Keeping these aims in view, debt management offices (DMOs) have been established in a number of countries particularly since the 1990s to manage public debt-maturity, volume of issue, other terms and conditions including the timing of the issues. The UK, the Euro area, the US, New Zealand, Singapore, Thailand, Malaysia, Australia, the Philippines, Russia, Vietnam and China have debt management agencies of different varieties. In this context, the following may be referred to. ECB Working Paper by Wolswijk and Haan (2005), Currie *et al.* (2003). In 2001, the IMF and World Bank prepared sound practice guidelines in respect of public debt management. This was published under the title, Guidelines for Public Debt Management. It was revised in December 2003. See the websites of the IMF and World Bank for the purpose. Also the IMF and the WB Staff paper (2007).

3. DMO within the Finance/Planning Ministry or outside as an independent organisation is an issue on which there is no unanimity of opinion. Though it is possible to have debt management functions entrusted to a private agency, this is rarely used by countries. It is sometimes argued that those countries that have separate debt management offices (i.e., outside the Ministry/Treasury) such as those in Austria, Ireland, Portugal, Sweden, Germany, Hungary and the UK often face the principal-agent relationship. On the other hand, so goes the argument, countries that have debt management functions undertaken within the Treasury/ Finance Ministry (examples being New Zealand, France, the Netherlands and Australia) try to contain fiscal risks and place portfolio management within the broader context of public policy. Whichever is the form, it is difficult to imagine how the principal-agency problem can be completely eschewed.

4. Owning shares of foreign banks could lead to lot of complex issues some of which relate to jurisdictions of national sovereignty and international legal positions. It is mainly for this reason, the Government of India did not nationalise the major foreign banks in India in the first wave of bank nationalisation in 1969. See the Reserve Bank of India (2006) and Patel (2002).

5. Measurement of seigniorage is not as easy as it is made out to be. Most monetary theorists used two different concepts of seigniorage while analysing its relationship with inflation. One of the concepts is the monetary seigniorage which is often measured in terms of the change in reserve money or monetary base deflated by the consumer price level. This was used by Friedman (1971), Cagan (1956), Fischer (1982), Calvo (1978), and Klein and Neumann (1990). The second concept is the opportunity cost seigniorage which is the total opportunity

costs for the holders of money. The real interest earnings foregone by the holders of money represent the opportunity cost. The best references to this concept are in Johnson (1969) and Barro (1982). The main point as to who gets the benefit of seigniorage that arises owing to printing of money may be seen from what might be called fiscal seigniorage which may be measured by deducting the government's deposits with the central bank from a sum of: (a) the central bank's holdings of government securities, (b) the interest received on such securities, (c) the interest received on the notes issued and (d) the coins issued net of expenditures of the mint. See Klein and Neumann (1990), Hochreiter and Rovelli (2001)

6. The Reserve Bank of India under its Act of 1934 established special funds for the promotion and development of agriculture and industry. The special funds were created out of the annual profits. They were for long-term and short-term operations. In the 1960s and 1970s, the Reserve Bank had established separate development institutions for industry and for agriculture and rural development. The Industrial Development Bank of India (IDBI) was hived off from the Reserve Bank of India in the 1970s while the National Bank for Agriculture and Rural Development (NABARD) was hived off from the Reserve Bank in the early 1980s. See for details, Reserve Bank of India (1998a) and Reserve bank of India (2006).

7. The Bank for International Settlements is entrusted with the task of providing the guidelines on surveillance on payments and settlements system. The Bank's standards and codes in this area are widely accepted as a good basis for IT applications that are compatible with the systems all over the global financial world. National authorities, however, have to undertake surveillance operations over both the national and international payments and settlements. This is also an area where the anti-money laundering issues come to the fore.

8. One can consider having Memoranda of Understandings (MoUs) between the governments and the central banks with regard to the monetisation of fiscal deficits and to the general loan and overdraft positions of the governments at the central banks. This is not uncommon. In India, such a MoU was signed between the Government of India and the Reserve Bank of India in 1997. See Reserve Bank of India (1998b) Annual Report.

9. Liquidity ratios are defined by central banks in quantifiable terms. In general, the securities considered as liquid are Federal Government securities. Liquidity ratio often functions as a prudential measure. From the point of view of long-term sound monetary governance, it is best that the content of liquidity for calculating the liquidity ratios of banks is not diluted mainly because such dilution would lead to market risks.

10. Having DMOs does not mean that debt management can be undertaken by the agency entrusted with it in an autonomous fashion without consulting the government and the central bank. The latter's critical input in debt management process may be seen from different angles. First, decisions about debt issuance will influence the quantum of the central bank's net credit to government and central bank credit to banks among others (such as net foreign exchange assets of the central bank and other credits of the central bank to other financial institutions and private sector bodies apart from net other assets). A large issue of government bonds could be absorbed by the central bank directly by participation in the auctions of government bonds at the time of the opening of the issues or through the credits provided to banks against the collateral of

government bonds. Net central bank credit to government is an important source of reserve money. Increased credits to commercial banks by the central banks against the collateral of government securities would, other things being equal, push up the reserve money. The second important critical input from the central bank would be regarding the timing of the new issues since most central banks are in touch with market conditions on a minute to minute basis. Thirdly, most central banks, notwithstanding their outward stance to the objective of growth, would still care about it simply because large scale borrowing operation will push up interest rates and reduce private investment through borrowing from the market. On the other hand, the fiscal authorities' influence on DMOs is more straightforward in that they could issue directives to DMOs to conduct the debt management operations to complete the budgeted estimates of public borrowing which one tends to believe would be based on fiscal sustainability analysis in most economies.

11. The difference between quantitative easing (QE) and credit easing (CE) was initiated by Fed chairman, Ben S. Bernanke, though it involved mere semantics with no guarantee that such a distinction would promote the public goods of price stability as well as of sound collateral policies in central banks. Bernanke claimed that the Federal Reserve's approach to supporting credit market is distinct, conceptually speaking, from quantitative easing and described the Fed approach as 'credit easing'. Both, however, imply that the balance sheet of the central bank would expand. Bernanke tried to explain the difference between QE and CE thus. In QE, the policy focus would be on the quantity of bank reserves whereas in CE, the focus would be on the mix of loans and securities that the central bank holds and how this composition of assets affects credit conditions. This is an artificial distinction since in both the cases the central bank balance sheet is increased. The basic point is that economic recovery is sought to be brought through actions that would have a bearing on the balance sheet of the central bank. See Bernanke (2009).

12. Discussions on Basle III norms had begun in right earnest from 2008 onwards. They can however be made operational only from January 01, 2013. From this date onwards, banks will have to meet minimum capital requirements expressed in risk-weighted assets in the following manner: 3.5 per cent share capital, 4.5 per cent Tier-1 capital and 8 per cent total capital. It is also agreed that there will be a transitional period to move towards full implementation. The transition period would stretch up to and including 2019. During this period, the ratios will be stepped up in a gradual manner to 4.5 per cent share capital, 6 per cent Tier-1 capital and 8 per cent total capital. There are also other requirements under the Basle III norms such as the conservation buffer, allowable deductions from bank capital to be introduced gradually by national supervisors, leverage ratio and the liquidity ratio. See for details, the website of the Bank for International Settlements.

13. Financial markets and financial instruments are under surveillance of the national authorities. In this connection, the IMF and the WB have been making joint assessments of the different areas of financial sector stability in the member countries and making them available to the national authorities for their closer examination of the issues that may need to be addressed in the near future. A comparative study of such individual country assessments requires to be made periodically particularly with regard to the desirability of continuing with or of

introducing a financial product. For instance, the debate on credit default swaps (CDSs) is a point on which countries that are interested in introducing it may be benefitted from such a comparative study.

14. It is important to note that the balance sheets of the central banks of both China and India expanded even before the global crisis emerged in 2007-08 mainly because of large scale capital inflows. This development was on account of relatively good growth performance of the two countries evoking confidence of investors, domestic and international. As a result, foreign exchange reserves of both the countries ballooned to levels not seen hitherto.

15. Discussions on the theory of sudden stops became fashionable since about the end of the 20th century after the international debt crisis of the 1980s and in particular, the Mexican crisis of 1994. This was subsequently revisited at the time of the East Asian crisis of 1997-98. For an account of sudden stops, see Calvo (2003), Calvo *et al.* (2004), Edwards (2005), Eichengreen *et al.* (2006), Montiel and Reinhart (1999) and Prati and Sbracia (2002).

16. The literature on information asymmetries is vast. See Akerlof (1970), Spence (1973, 1974) and Stiglitz and Weiss (1981) for the initial contributions. The asymmetric information in credit markets has led to articles that provided insights on economic policy and lending practices. See Bebczuk (2003). Mankiw (1986) showed that information frictions and credit market failures that arise thereby can create inefficiency through underinvestment. Bernanke and Gertler (1990) point out the possible overinvestment taking place owing to inefficiency arising from credit market failures. From the policy point of view, the information asymmetry leading to adverse selection could be met to a significant extent by subsidies, loan guarantees, appropriately designed coordination of information and improved screening processes. But there is very little empirical literature identifying the information asymmetries and the frictions that they cause.

17. A notable exception is India which had in early 2000s constituted a number of working groups on the standards and codes that different financial markets and institutions should adopt keeping in view the legal and institutional constraints and the need to be consistent with the broadly accepted international standards and codes. The members in these working groups were drawn not only from the Ministry of Finance and Reserve Bank of India but also from the market and from the academic circles. Reference may be made to the website of the Reserve Bank of India to get necessary details at: *www.rbi.org.in*

18. The costs of forbearance cannot be easily measured. Failure to enforce mandated capital standards in banks and other financial institutions is one instance of forbearance. Forbearance also arises when the authorities allow extension of time for payments of dues (either on account of principal repayments or interest payments), or when income recognition norms are relaxed. In case forbearance is not applied and the firm (bank or any other financial institution) fails, there could be spillover and contagion effects on the rest of the financial sector. More often than not, the governments intervened to support the financial institutions when they were under severe financial stress. This has been particularly the case after the failure of the Lehman Brothers in 2007 in New York, United States.

19. There are some efforts by Ross Levine and his colleagues to sort out this matter through simple regression analysis. Their work in 2006 may be read along with

Ross Levine's paper submitted to the Conference at Jackson Hole in August 2011. See Barth *et al.* (2006) and Levine (2011).

20. The 'too big to fail' argument has been squarely criticised by every analyst ever since 2007. The big and highly diversified banks are supposed to: (a) enjoy the benefits of scale economies, (b) generate efficiency gains mainly through scale economies to a substantial extent and (c) generate high risk-adjusted returns which in turn provide scope for market valuation to go up. But recent empirical analysis does not provide much evidence of the presence of scale economies in international banking. See BIS (2010). Nor is there good support for market valuation going up when returns are risk-adjusted. See Laeven and Levine (2007).

21. Credit default swaps (CDS) are credit derivatives. A credit derivative contract is between two counterparties. The buyer of the contract makes periodic payments to the seller of the contract and in return receives a pay off, if an underlying financial instrument defaults or experiences a similar credit event. The CDS may refer to a specified loan or bond obligation of a reference entity, the entity being either the government or a corporation. Credit event in the case of a corporation could include outright default, or failure to pay, or restructuring and bankruptcy. In the case of sovereign, credit event could include repudiation, moratorium and acceleration. Reliable data on CDS are not available despite the many good attempts made by the Bank for International Settlements.

22. Collateralised debt obligations (CDOs) refer to a structured asset-backed security. In order to create a CDO, a corporation has to be constructed to hold assets as collateral and sell packages of cash flows to investors. This takes usually the following form. A special purpose entity (SPE) is designed first to acquire a portfolio of underlying assets—mortgage-backed securities, commercial real estate bonds and corporate loans. The SPE will issue bonds to investors in exchange for cash which is used to purchase a portfolio of underlying assets. The bonds issued are layers with different risk characteristics. Senior tranches are paid from the cash flows from the underlying assets before the junior securities and equity securities. Losses will be borne first by the equity securities, next by the junior tranches and finally by the senior tranches. Data on CDOs are also not as reliable as is made out to be.

4

The Analytics and Communications

Monetary governance to be credible should have fiscal and monetary policies set on sound analytical framework. It is often taken for granted that the frameworks of the two policies are based on the economic realities of the countries in question. The connect between the analytics and the economic realities is supposed to be provided by the recent trend of governments and central banks to make use of the new technologies that are available to them for receiving feedback of the soundness of their proposed analytics. What this means is that aspects of what the frameworks contain, what they are intended to achieve and how they are expected to be put into effect would be placed on their websites for comment from the public. The reactions are supposed to provide feedback on the theoretical soundness and practicality of the frameworks being designed. The consultative process implied in this approach has an in-built incentive to the authorities to explain as to how their decisions are arrived at and how far the decisions are framework-based. It does give scope for supplementing analytics with judgments of the circumstances in which the countries are placed. The information provided in the process need not be just statistical in nature but it will surely be knowledge-centric. By explaining the rationale of the decisions, the authorities will be transparent that is critical for effective monetary governance. Transparency in turn entails accountability. Such an open approach on the part of the authorities would prima facie influence the behaviour of economic participants and to improve market expectations.[1]

Analytics of Fiscal Policy

The analytical framework for good governance by the fiscal authorities has to be based on what the society desires the government to do. The society's preferences are supposed to be better represented in democracies since the representatives of societies that are elected to parliaments and legislative assemblies through legislative actions would reflect the role that the state/government would play in economic and social spheres of activity. However, enactments by legislatures consisting of people's representatives are often in general terms. Good governance would require that the state's role be codified in detail and that the codified provisions are fully implemented for gaining credibility. To be more specific, should there be well designed fiscal policy rules in place? Or should the governments, instead of having strict rules, be allowed to use discretion in fiscal management to counter cyclical changes in the economy? The latter is what most governments would prefer because of the flexibility it affords. However, discretion, as Kydland and Prescott (1977) have argued, could be time inconsistent and could provide a means of reneging on the announced policy commitments. Cukierman and Meltzer (1986) pointed out that discretion allows governments that seek to improve their electability or re-electability to use suboptimal discretionary policies that may not necessarily lead to maximum social welfare. In other words, discretion affords politicisation of fiscal policy.

Fiscal policy framework when laid down in the form of rules entails specification of certain indicators or targets along with enunciation of principles of transparency. This does not mean that there will be no clauses that permit deviation from the specified target in the event of unforeseen exogeneous shocks such as sharply adverse terms of trade, natural calamities and cyclical swings in activity. Such deviations have become more frequent and sharply experienced in many EMEs with the growing economic globalisation. This point has come into sharp focus with EMEs and developing countries experiencing severe shocks owing to the financial crisis that erupted first in the US and in the IEs and in the rest of the world. This led many emerging and developing countries to give up their fiscal commitments and targets and provide stimulus in order to preserve growth momentum during the year 2009 and a part of 2010. What is pertinent to recognise is that deviations cannot be easily corrected within a short period of time, particularly if the order of fiscal stimulus had been large as was the case in respect of many emerging and developing economies in 2008 and a part of 2009. It is also important that for understanding the interaction between the public sector and the general economy, it is necessary to make estimates of the response of the fiscal position to exogeneous shocks, as argued by Kopits (2001). Such estimates could be mandated while designing the fiscal rules, in view of the fact that global integration of economies cannot be avoided. Such rules will then help serve as transparency practices.

It must, however, be recognised that advocacy for rigid rules without escape clauses and without any transparency would be as dangerous as unconditional or complete discretion. Constrained discretion is what is needed but it should be used in a prudent manner. However, as judgments about the infallibility of 'prudent' use of discretion could be faulty, it would be pragmatic to have flexible application of fiscal rules with indicative benchmarks instead of iron-cast targets.

Fiscal policy framework under such a flexible rule regime may be viewed in terms of two major blocs. One would be on macro-economic stabilisation in the context of growth and the other would be on fiscal responsibility. Both complement each other. The stabilisation policy bloc will consist of the calculation of the fiscal deficit/surplus, borrowing and debt. The fiscal responsibility bloc will generally be in the form of legislation that focusses on the management of the stocks of financial assets generated by the stabilisation policy bloc.

In the stabilisation bloc there will be a cluster of rules in the form of a large number of indicators/benchmarks/targets along with the necessary escape clauses. The bloc could confine itself to laying down the rules for the immediate year ahead or for a medium term of 3-5 years ahead. The medium-term framework will provide a trajectory with the end-period indicative benchmark that could be sustained in the absence of any unforeseen shock. Sustainability will mean that there would be no deliberate fiscal deficit bias to meet either pro-cyclical needs or development needs. The benchmark will again be used as a reference point for analysis and for implementation and not as a rigid rule estimate. The sustainable medium-term trajectory will, by definition, be a product of short-term benchmarks.

Fiscal deficits rather than balanced budget rules are, however, the preferred option in EMEs provided the deficits are sustainable. For this purpose, estimations of tax revenues need to be worked out and expenditures set along with estimations of output gap.[2] In some countries, revenues are mainly from one or two natural resources (such as copper, crude oil) in which case they could be subject to fluctuations relating to price cycles or external shocks in trading partner countries. The normal practice in countries with high dependence on one or two natural resources would be to protect government spending from the effects of economic cycles as well as of natural resource price cycles through creation of special stabilisation funds.

Whatever be the ultimate fiscal position, deficit or surplus, it is important to explain the rules underlying the framework and the risk factors in achieving a benchmark of overall deficit/surplus. Two or three risk factors may need to be kept in view. One is the net worth of central banks which might issue debts when they take on the debt of commercial banks thereby causing negative or sharp fall in their annual operating incomes. The second risk factor would be the contingent fiscal liabilities incurred on account of the guarantees that governments provide. Finally, there is the risk of experiencing external vulnerability either due to commitment of the 'original sin', the original sin being on account of incurring debt in foreign currency, or the deterioration in external competitiveness owing to country's high production costs of exportable commodities.

Once the fiscal position is worked out, it would be possible to estimate the borrowing needs and the debt position. Fiscal policy sustainability would hinge largely on the sustainability of public debt, expressed in relation to GDP. In this context, debt composition, low roll-over risk, and growth prospects are some of the elements that are monitored. The interest payments paid out every year on the outstanding debt matters a great deal especially if the debt is denominated in foreign currency and if there are exchange rate fluctuations. Given the debt, it is important to work out the total servicing payments (on account of debt redemption and interest payments). Interest payments in particular are paid out of the revenue account of the budgets and as such primary deficits (arrived at by deducting the interest payments from the overall fiscal deficit) assume importance in the fiscal sustainability exercise. Primary deficit needs to be nil or negligible to ensure that the debt level is stable. Countries with high debt levels would be liable to interest rate shocks as well as growth shocks and would not be able to ensure that public debt is sustainable. To get at the overall fiscal sustainability, it is essential to monitor indicators such as the fiscal deficit/surplus to GDP; the revenue or current deficit to GDP; the primary deficit to GDP; the total borrowing in a year; the yearly interest payments and principal repayments and the debt to GDP ratio.

In some emerging countries, the modes of financing of fiscal deficit matter a great deal, particularly if the central banks are required to finance fiscal deficit.[3] There is also a need to ensure that revenue or current deficit is avoided so that the current surpluses would help finance capital expenditures especially those that give high social rates of return as in the case of infrastructure projects. Besides, the fiscal rules should be not only at the national level but also at the subnational level, so that the consolidated national fiscal position would provide a meaningful picture of the consolidated financial position of the public sector of the country. In some countries where public sector enterprises both at the Federal and sub-national levels exist, it is important to ensure that they function efficiently without relying on bailouts or bridge financing from the government.[4] Such an approach requires that institutional arrangements are in place to coordinate the intent and actions of the Federal Government and subnational governments.

The stabilisation policy bloc must also have rules consisting of institutional requirements for compliance and for laying down transparency standards in reporting. Most countries have constitutional provisions for institutions that report on individual ministries' expenditures and accounting policies and submit them for parliamentary approval. Non-compliance to rules and policies often leads to public sanction and legal suits against the errant officials including cabinet ministers. Rules concerning the working of the institutions would need to be designed for good monetary governance.

The fiscal responsibility bloc will essentially ensure that there are funds to manage the stocks of financial assets. There could be stabilisation funds for different activities such as agricultural and industrial operations. In countries which rely substantially on crude oil sales, there could be stabilisation fund created out of surpluses in oil budget in order to protect the oil industry from the impact of adverse price/demand shocks in certain years. Stabilisation funds could also be in the form of pension reserve funds and their investments tend to be generally in the domestic economy. The portfolio choice and portfolio growth tend to affect domestic financial markets. In order to shield the exchange rate and local financial asset markets from the effects of fiscal portfolio growth, surpluses or accumulations in reserve funds may have to be invested abroad.

It is necessary to have rules laid down in respect of the functioning of the various funds in the public sector so that they do not impinge on the fiscal stabilisation policy. These rules could be a part of the fiscal responsibility enactments. However, the enactments should also provide for requisite time horizons for applicability of rules and provisions to meet shocks and other unavoidable circumstances.

How does one make sure that fiscal governance is effective? This can be done only empirically and individually for each country. In general, debt sustainability analysis is taken as a good basis for evaluating the fiscal sustainability. The earliest rule of debt sustainability was provided by Domar (1944). Under this rule, debt sustainability is obtained when growth rate is higher than or at least equal to the real rate of interest. Buiter (1985) and subsequently Blanchard *et al.* (1990) provided a framework based on the government inter-temporal budget constraint and suggested two sustainability conditions, *viz.*, convergence of the debt to GDP ratio in the long run to its initial level and equalisation of the present value of the ratio of primary budget deficit to GDP with the negative of the current level of public debt to GDP. A number of other studies (Ghosh *et al.*, 2011; Bohn, 1998; Abiad and Ostry, 2005) dealt with sustainable public debt and came out with models and empirical results that dealt with advanced and emerging countries. In general they pointed to the need for primary balance to be positive and sufficient enough to ensure that the long-run public debt does not take an explosive path, going beyond the stable level.

Analytics of Monetary Policy

The monetary policy framework relevant for good monetary governance is essentially about the operating procedures of monetary policy. The theoretical underpinnings of monetary policy are well known: they relate to monetary targetting of the very classical variety or of a nuanced form, exchange rate targetting, interest rate targetting and inflation targetting. On monetary policy rules, the essence of the theoretical structure can be captured from a few articles such as those of Friedman (1960) and Taylor (1993) and from the numerous analytical and empirical articles on the transmission channels of monetary policy.[5] These provide the rationale for the actions of central banks.

In recent years, much of the discussion on monetary policy is conducted in terms of inflation targetting or interest rate targetting. Exchange rate targetting is essentially confined in scope: they are seen in only two open economies, namely, Singapore and Hong Kong. Monetary targetting of the typically classical variety has already been given up essentially because of: (a) the well proved instability in money demand, as Poole (1970) had so correctly suggested and (b) financial innovations. Interest rate targetting has never been an independent framework *per se*, simply because interest rate is the variable that is implicitly targetted whether the policy framework is described as monetary targetting or inflation targetting. The transmission effects that follow from the interest rate channel could be described in the following manner. Consider the monetary policy action say open market operation (OMO) affecting the reserve balances. It influences both rate and quantity variables. It impacts the short-term interest rate and through it other market interest rates. The quantity variable that is influenced would be the reserve money or central bank money and through it the money supply via the money multiplier. Money supply in its turn influences the market interest rate. The market interest rate will have impact on the real interest rate. It is the real interest rate that will eventually impact the aggregate demand. It is indeed the real interest rate impact on aggregate demand that is the quintessence of interest rate channel of monetary policy.

Monetary targetting has lost much of its ground owing to instability in money demand. The one framework that has become available to the authorities is, prima facie, inflation targetting. But inflation targetting too has not proved to be reliable, from the empirical works on transmission channels of monetary policy relating to emerging and developing economies. The effects of policy changes, particularly when they are frequent as has been the case in most EMEs during 2009 and 2010, on transmission channels have made inflation targetting an unreliable policy rule or even framework. Post recent crisis, it has become apparent that price stability does not foster financial stability and growth impulses. Jobless growth has coexisted with low inflation. Low or almost zero-bound interest rates did not trigger growth impulses. Financial institutions continued to experience stresses and strains even when growth was low, unemployment high and inflation low. These outcomes in major IEs (in particular the US, the UK and many European economies during the years 2009-2011) show that inflation targetting as a framework is not necessarily best suited to emerging economies. On the analytical plane, there is also the major problem of measuring output gaps in many an emerging economy which is at the heart of inflation targetting and the Taylor-type rule.

Irrespective of the label that one gives to policy framework, what most central banks do as a matter of course, is to announce the official policy rate of interest. This announcement is made whether the ultimate objectives of policy are confined to a single one or to a dual or a multiple set. The announced policy rate is supposed to affect the deposit and lending rates of banks which in turn influence the spending decisions of economic agents. The spending decisions could pertain to consumption spending and/or investment spending. The policy rate is the rate for the short period and will in turn influence other short-term rates of interest such those on inter-bank transactions and medium- and long-term rates of interest especially those on long-term bonds of 10-year and over 10-year duration. To put it simply, the official rate is said to influence the term structure of interest rates or the yield curve.

In order to ensure that the announced policy rate has the requisite effect, it is necessary for the central bank to track a market rate of interest that influences spending decisions of economic agents. The market rate of interest that is required to be tracked would be the operational target of central banks. More often than not, the operational target would be the rate in the inter-bank call market. The inter-bank call rate, by definition, would be the uncollateralised rate and would therefore carry a risk premium.

Some banks, however, may need to access funds in the inter-bank market to meet the funding requirements of their loan and investment managers that go beyond the banks' own (deposit) resources. In such circumstances, banks could access funds from the inter-bank market on overnight basis at a rate that would be higher than the rate of interest that central banks charge on their overnight loans to banks. If the inter-bank market rates are high and are way ahead of the central banks' rate on their loans, there will not be any incentive for banks to enter the inter-bank market as borrowers. No doubt central banks charge rates of interest on their loans at rates that are higher than the announced policy rates, against the lodgement of specified collateral securities. Banks that have surplus funds can park their funds with the central bank which as a rule pay a rate of interest that will be lower than the policy rate. The central banks' lending rates and deposit rates are thus determined with reference to the policy rate and they thus represent the upper and lower bounds. It is the corridor of interest rates that authorities determine with reference to the objective of reducing the volatility in the inter-bank call rates and confining the rate movement within the corridor.

It is not that once the corridor of interest rate is determined, inter-bank call rates will on their own settle to the expected pattern. In fact, to ensure that the operational target would stay in the middle of the corridor or stable within the corridor, central banks would conduct liquidity operations (open market operations and repo operations in the main). In this context, two issues arise. How much should be the width of the corridor? This question may be answered in terms of the stage of development of the financial markets. In economies with developed financial markets, the corridor would be narrow and would be of a width of 100 basis points. In developing economies with less developed financial markets, the width of the corridor would be larger and this would help improve the development of the financial markets. The second question is: should the corridor be symmetric? Cannot central banks consider asymmetric corridors especially when banks hesitate to enter the unsecured inter-bank market? In general, there has been a preference for symmetry of the corridor though under certain circumstances, asymmetry is justifiable.[6] The circumstances that central banks faced during the recent financial crisis, in particular during 2009, however, recognised the criticality of this issue. The idea behind the proposal for asymmetry is that it will penalise reserve build up at the central bank and encourage borrowing by banks and help improve liquidity management and inter-bank liquidity market.

There is no hard and fast rule that one should have a corridor of interest rates, symmetric or asymmetric. It is possible as a result of the recent financial crisis to implement monetary policy with a narrow passive corridor or without a corridor as is done by a number of central banks in IEs (ECB, Bank of Japan, Bank of England, Bank of Canada, Norges Bank and the Reserve Bank of New Zealand). The new system is the floor system. In this framework, the operational target and the floor rate that is paid on bank reserves or on excess reserves would converge. The floor rate system has come into being essentially because the central banks had to supply more reserve balances to stabilise financial markets. It would, however, offer limited incentives for inter-bank trading. The very narrow passive corridor—something like ±15 basis points—will not be in practice much different from a floor rate system. However, it is not yet well established that the floor rate system is optimal for all times—normal or unstable or stressed situations. It is to be seen whether the central banks would consider the floor rate system to be temporary and suited to meet particular demands of financial stress and revert to corridor system once the economies recover completely from the ongoing financial and economic crisis.[7] Intuitively speaking, the system that encourages inter-bank trading is what is desirable since it may be expected to foster financial market stability in normal times.

The floor system may not be the only alternative to the corridor system. One could theoretically think of having a ceiling system in place of the floor or corridor system. In such an event, the rate that the central banks would charge for overnight lending against collateral will act as a guide for borrowers in the uncollateralised inter-bank market. Under this framework, the bank rate or the official rate may be used selectively and in specified amounts for certain categories of borrowers such as the Federal Government. An excess of the uncollateralised inter-bank rate over the central bank lending rate would represent risk premium. If the risk premium is high, it will signal to policymakers of the risks to banks that may arise due to adverse selection. Monetary policy then would have to be triggered to signal the need to keep credit growth under check through not necessarily the rate changes or changes in liquidity requirements and could well be through structural changes as such. For example, the exposure limits of commercial banks to certain borrowing sectors could be moved up in cases where credit growth seems to pose high market risks.

The fourth type of framework could be what may be called for want of a better term, eclectic, typically in the American tradition of Canada prior to the 1990s and of the US till almost the end of Alan Greenspan era. Among the EMEs, the one example of eclectic framework is of India which officially states its position as 'multiple indicator' approach. This approach has been in vogue in India since 1998. Its quintessence has been brought out in a number of reports of the Reserve Bank of India, especially its Annual Reports. The approach based as it is on multiple indicators, places emphasis on the central bank exerting constrained discretion, constrained in that it is used in consultation with the government and in close monitoring of the views of financial sector participants, in respect of a number of elements. One of them is about the choice of the objective to be given priority in conducting policy at the given point in time, from among the set of objectives, without forsaking the rest of the objectives. The second relates to the choice of the policy instrument, especially the one that will have impact on the Government of India's debt management and exchange rate policies. The third element is concerned with efforts at coordination with other regulators as well as the Government of India in respect of financial sector development and regulation.

How does the eclectic approach work? India's approach is operated beginning with the announcement of the operational target—the inter-bank call rate—as well as the corridor—narrow often within 100-150 basis points—of interest rates under the repo operations. OMO is resorted to in order to ensure that the operational target moves within the corridor, not necessarily at the centre of the corridor. This has been widely regarded as a good enough effective performance of monetary policy by market analysts and economists. While the eclectic approach has the advantage of a wide intuitive appeal, it could be abused if economic governance is weak or if the Treasury is too powerful and too obsessed with the logic of pursuing its own objectives. The floor system which came into being mainly because of the financial crisis of 2007-08, does not provide the guarantee of its useful in normal times. The ceiling system has been in vogue in many countries for a long time till the system of the corridor system came into being. The corridor system can be a part of the eclectic approach as well. The only question that remains to be addressed is one that relates to the designing of the corridor. Where financial market development is not completely free from risks and where financial markets are relatively less developed, it would probably be prudent to adopt a corridor, with its width being determined by judgment about the degree of development of the financial markets. However, it is important to recognise that the larger the width, the higher the scope for manipulation by a few strong banks in the financial system. Small banks with limited liquid assets in their portfolios will be forced to pay high rates in the inter-bank call market when they are faced with shortage of market funding liquidity.

Assume for a while, the corridor system is in operation in an emerging economy. Assume also that the inter-bank call rate is the operational target. Suppose on a particular day, the call rate is within the corridor but not at or close to the centre of the corridor on a particular day or for a week. Suppose the call rate is very close to the upper band. What should the central bank do? Should it inject liquidity or be prepared to inject liquidity? The simple answer, going by the received wisdom, would be that the central bank should be prepared to inject liquidity whenever call rates move above the centre of the corridor. However, one could determine the liquidity injection only when the rate moves above the centre not on any one day but on a specified number of days and at some point away from the upper band. For instance, if the call rate moves to the upper band with only 5 per cent of the width of the corridor left to touch the ceiling rate for not one day but for 3-4 days, one could consider it a decision point triggering action to inject liquidity. Similarly, when the call rate is below the lower band or very close to the lower band within the corridor, the central bank should be prepared to absorb liquidity under a determined decision point-trigger. However, there is a caveat in the determination of the decision points. It is that when the movement of the call rate does not reflect the system liquidity issue but only a funding liquidity issue for a particular bank or a group of banks (say the small-sized banks), the central bank will have to willy-nilly take measures to tackle the funding liquidity issues of the relevant bank or group of banks.

Central banks generally work out liquidity requirements of banks on a day to day basis through what is often called the liquidity forecasting exercises. The liquidity forecasting exercises have become standardised templates. The exercise essentially points to the need to make a judgment as to how much of reserves should be supplied by the central bank to meet the banks' demand for reserves. Forecasting for the period ahead, usually for the following fortnight or month is done at least once a day, normally at the beginning of the working hours. These forecasts are matched with the information collected by market intelligence sources regarding market developments. The forecasts thus are not pure technical exercises. They are adjusted estimates with the latest market information inputted into them. It is only then the central bank managements make a judgment call as to whether reserves should be supplied or withdrawn and if so by what amounts and in what manner. The reserves that central banks supply are thus 'discretionary' or 'policy' liquidity.

Discretionary liquidity is generally provided through the use of conventional policy instruments. Such instruments consist of repo or open market operations, reserve requirements, the rate at which overnight loans are provided by central banks to those banks that seek such facility, the rate that the central bank would pay for the deposits parked with it by banks on overnight basis and the interventions in the foreign exchange market. During the recent financial crisis, however, discretionary liquidity has been provided also through the use of what have known to be 'unconventional' policy measures. These took a variety of forms: asset repurchase programmes, establishing swap lines with foreign central banks for increasing foreign currency liquidity, establishing somewhat longer-term credit lines for banks, and setting up special credit facilities for term securities lending or commercial paper funding.

Liquidity management is undoubtedly a critical part of the operating procedures of monetary policy. But it does not mean that it will necessarily help achieve the ultimate objectives of monetary policy. Most importantly, liquidity management by monetary authorities can become a severe challenge if the coordination between the fiscal and monetary authorities is suboptimal and/or if foreign capital flows are subjected to sudden shocks. External shocks are not within control but the shocks from fiscal operations can be influenced through central banks reaching out to governments on the extent of fiscal liquidity that fiscal operations would generate in the week/month ahead and the implications thereof for the market rates of interest. The consultative process would help understand the influence that interest rate would wield on consumption and investment demand that would ultimately have impact on prices and output.

The Context of the Crisis

The consultative process was in evidence during the recent financial crisis in both IEs and EMEs in that the fiscal and monetary stimulus were undertaken to address the issues posed by financial stress and sudden dip in economic prospects. Interestingly enough, the considerations were slightly nuanced as between the two groups of countries. In IEs, financial fragility and economic recession were the issues to be addressed, not so much the issue of price stability. The stimulus in IEs was a part of pushing up aggregate demand with clear intention of bolstering and facilitating economic activities including infrastructure services. It was expected that such a stimulus would help generate employment push up aggregate supply. This process would ensure that both growth and price stability would be achieved.

In EMEs, however, the stimulus was intended to bolster domestic demand in order to compensate the loss of external demand arising from the economic recession in their trading partners, particularly among the IES. This strategy was evolved essentially because EMEs have been on the high growth cycle at the time of the emergence of the global economic crisis. The actions of EMEs are thus intended to protect and preserve the growth momentum. The actions also imply that the ill-effects of global economic integration could be attenuated at least partially by a bit of decoupling from the embrace of the IEs. The rise in domestic demand, however, has generated inflation pressures. In some cases, the inflationary pressures were accentuated by large capital inflows. As a result EMEs in general and China and India in particular, had to face higher than tolerable rates of inflation. Countering inflation has opened up the inevitable question of working out an acceptable short run trade-off between growth and inflation. EMEs have been compelled to devise strategies to reconcile the trade-off after a determination is made to exit from the domestic stimulus in a calibrated manner. The exit strategy meant that both fiscal consolidation and monetary tightening would have to go hand in hand in a measured way through consultative processes.

The recent global crisis has thrown up a global economic model that was hitherto not recognised in economic literature. The model in which industrialised economies would lead the rest of the world has been overturned with emerging and many developing countries recording high growth rates and helping to propel the global economic activity at a fairly high level. Among the emerging countries, the most mentioned are Brazil, China and India. But it must be recognised that many developing countries in Latin America and Africa have also registered high growth rates in recent years.[8] But this model of IEs piggy-backing on the growth of EMEs is not sustainable. This is because the saving and investment rates and institutional and structural adjustments required of emerging and developing countries to enable the IEs' returning to the growth trajectory of the pre-crisis years would be highly burdensome. The rainbow of interests of both governments and monetary authorities at the international level would suggest that IEs have to undertake strong economic adjustment to return to pre-crisis levels.

Communication: Key to Understanding the Analytics

Explaining the analytical frameworks in simple language is necessary in all societies, irrespective of the level of economic literacy. Besides, it is important to explain the policy stance, the rationale of the decisions taken and the implementation strategies that are designed at each point of policy formulation for promoting monetary governance. This would not be possible if there is no communications policy. Such a policy should be stated clearly and should be imbued with transparency and accountability. The literature on communications policy, however, is largely biased towards monetary policy in most economies. In so far as fiscal policy is concerned, communications are generally in the form of legislative enactments, budget documents and official announcements, though there are internationally known transparency practices in fiscal policy.[9] The legal enactments and the fiscal transparency practices, as set in IEs and many EMEs have not necessarily led to open communication, notwithstanding the fact that public availability of information which is a part of the transparency practice could in societies with relatively high economic literacy lead to mid-course policy corrections. Most economists prefer fiscal rules to discretionary fiscal policy. There is also no agreement among economists that automatic stabilisers would work best in all economic circumstances. It is when the financial crisis erupted in 2007 and has escalated in 2008, fiscal stimulus was undertaken not under any laid-down rule but as a temporary measure as part of discretion of the governments to bring about quick economic recovery.[10] When economic data of major IEs at the end of 2010 seemed to suggest that economic recovery is on way, though at a low speed, a number of questions arose about fiscal sustainability, the high debt to GDP ratios, the impact of fiscal policy and the burden that high fiscal stimulus has imposed on societies. Many IEs are aware that the burden is so high that fiscal correction will take a lot more time to yield the desired results but in the meantime, social protests against retrenchment of workers are growing up, with possibility of their taking a sharp tone. Whether the difficult political situation in some IEs could be assuaged by bailouts by countries that are relatively in a better economic position is a matter on which there is no finality of judgment. It is also not clear whether communication of fiscal consolidation strategy for the medium term of 3-5 years to overcome the present impasse would be considered as credible so long as the unemployment rate is higher than what could be considered as tolerable. It is just not enough to focus on the uncertainties of the effects of fiscal policy-tax breaks and expenditure changes and their effects on the real economy and their indirect effects on monetary policy decisions through their influence on inflation expectations, as many discussions in the economic literature since about the middle of 2011 have tended to focus upon. Unemployment is the main issue now.

As against the somewhat muted tone in the literature on the communication policies and strategies relating to fiscal policies, there is considerable literature on monetary policy on the question of communications of central banks.[11] Most central banks believe that communications play a crucial role in signalling their policy intentions. Some central banks have even presented their communication policies on their websites.[12] However, most policy statements are rarely presented in simple understandable language and are, more often than not, couched in a language that can be characterised as constructive ambiguity. This is what should be avoided scrupulously by the authorities since it has the potential of ultimately leading to considerable loss of credibility and lack of public confidence in the effectiveness of policies that are enunciated or are being enunciated.

The Message

The institutions that are required to be set up for good monetary governance would have to be led by good analytical frameworks of both the fiscal and monetary authorities. Without frameworks and some ground rules, even if they are flexibly adopted, fiscal and monetary actions are likely to be inconsistent, with potential of causing considerable confusion at the market place and among the wider public. Sound communication policies and strategies would help reduce misunderstanding of the focus and rationale of policies but they would not be credible if the fiscal and monetary policy makers do not fine tune their analytical frameworks to the needs of the economy and consult each other for marrying them together for purposes of macroeconomic balance together with the setting up of effective institutional mechanisms.

End Notes

1. It must however be recognised that in certain circumstances when economic uncertainty is sharp, the authorities may have to make judgment calls rather than applying rigidly the analytical frameworks available to them. It is also possible they may not be able to empirically prove the soundness of their judgments. If the authorities are perceived to have relied too much on their judgments, they will be damned for not being sufficiently faithful to their own theoretical framework. If, on the other hand, they do not want to make any judgments and follow the analytics as text books tend to suggest, they would be damned for not being sensitive to the economic and social realities that are apparently clearly visible or well known. Either way, the policymakers are likely to be damned.

2. Output gap provides the difference between what is viewed as potential output and actual output. It is written thus: Ya-Yp, where Ya is actual output and Yp is potential output. If Ya>Yp, it means that aggregate demand is in excess of aggregate supply. Such a situation could indicate the possible emergence of inflation. Measurement of potential output, however, poses a serious problem in many developing economies. This problem has been surmounted to a good extent in recent years in some of the EMEs.

3. Regarding the central bank financing of government deficit, the Indian experience is most fascinating. The monetisation of the fiscal deficit by the Reserve Bank of India was a distinct feature right from the middle of the 1950s to the end of March 1997 through the issuance of what is known as ad hoc Treasury bills. Ad hoc Treasury bills were issued whenever the balances of the Government of India with the Reserve Bank of India as at the end of Fridays were lower than the agreed minimum balance of Rs 50 crore, a crore being equivalent of 10 million. The ad hoc bills were cancelled as soon as the balances reach the agreed level of Rs 500 million. Originally, the arrangement as agreed to between the Government of India and the Reserve Bank of India was to be a temporary one but over time, it became more or less a regular feature till it was dismantled at the end of March 1997 by a memorandum of understanding between the two parties in question. The interest rate on ad hocs was the same as that on regular treasury bills. For details of this experience, see Vasudevan (2003). The dismantling of the idea of automatic monetisation of fiscal deficit was largely due to the efforts of C. Rangarajan, who joined the Reserve Bank of India first as Deputy Governor in 1982 and became Governor of the Reserve Bank of India in December 1992. See Rangarajan *et al.* (1989) and Rangarajan (1993). See also for automatic monetisation of deficit, the history volume of the Reserve Bank of India (1998a).

4. The PSBR concept essentially provides such a picture. The PSBR concept is useful in that it provides an idea of the future saving outcomes which, as is well known, serves as the best basis for investment planning.

5. A large number of articles have appeared on the transmission channels of monetary policy since the early 1970s. A good summary position of all the transmission channels may be obtained from Mishkin (1995).

6. See Goodhart (2009) and Quiros and Mendizabal (2009).

7. See for a discussion on interest rate corridors, the recent monetary frameworks and the floor rate systems, Whitesell (2006), Engert *et al.* (2008), ECB (2008),

Bank of England (2008, 2011), Kahn (2010) and Bernhardsen and Kloster (2010). For treatment of the way monetary policy is conducted, see Mohanty (2011).

8. The data made available by the IMF (2011b) on the world output is very interesting. The average output growth for 1993-2002 for advanced economies was 2.8 per cent: it was more or less stable at 2.7 per cent in the period 2003-07. It slumped to an average of -1.8 per cent during the crisis years 2008-09. There was perceptible recovery in output growth to 3.1 per cent in 2010 but the latest figure for 2010 places the likely growth to be 1.6 per cent. The US which posted average growth of 2.7 per cent during the period 2003-2007 posted a negative average growth of 1.6 per cent in the crisis years 2008-09. In 2010, the growth in the US recovered to 3.0 per cent. In 2011, however, it is placed at 1.6 per cent. The emerging and developing economies posted an excellent average growth of 7.6 per cent in the period 2003-2007. In the crisis years 2008-09, the average growth decelerated to 4.4 per cent. In 2010, there was some recovery in output growth to 7.3 per cent. It is expected to decelerate further to 6.4 per cent in 2011. The Asian growth story is by far better having posted an average of 7.5 per cent in the crisis years of 2008-09 as against 9.6 per cent in the period 2003-2007. However, it is expected that growth in Asia would be fairly robust at 8.2 per cent in 2011. Sub-Saharan Africa which posted an average growth of 6.3 per cent in 2003-2007 decelerated to 4.2 per cent during the two crisis years of 2008-09. In 2010, SSA grew by 5.4 per cent and is likely to post a growth of 5.2 per cent in 2011. There is a general recognition that the world economy would slow down markedly in 2011 due to lack of confidence in policymaking in advanced economies in general and in European economies in particular. See for detailed analysis IMF (2011b).
9. The Committee of the Board of Governors adopted the Code of Good Practices on Fiscal Transparency: Declaration on Principles on April 16, 1998. It was reviewed subsequently and the review was approved by the IMF Board in 2007. The Code is based on four general principles: (a) clarity of roles and responsibilities; (b) open budget processes; (c) public availability of information and (d) assurances of integrity. The IMF basing itself on these four general principles issued a Manual on Fiscal Transparency (2007).
10. See Spilimbergo *et al.* (2008); Taylor (2000) and (2009).
11. See for good references, Bank for International Settlements (2009); Blinder *et al.* (2008); Dincer *et al.* (2009); Woodford (2005); Kahn (2007) and Mohan (2005).
12. See the Reserve Bank of India website for a detailed exposition of communication policy. *<http://www.rbi.org.in>*

5

The International Dimension

The international dimension of monetary governance, referred to here as international or global monetary governance, implies that governments and central banks would be the main actors in addressing issues that confront the international monetary and financial system. As governments and central banks interact with other financial regulators for the overall good of their domestic economies, one could assume that financial regulators' concerns would be proxied when they enter into discussions on international monetary governance. At the global level, governance will necessarily exude the colour and richness of international economic diplomacy. To the extent the major multilateral institutions represent the financial arm of such a diplomacy, the IMF and the WB get involved in the discussions. This is reflected in the fact that the number of G-20 meetings at the levels of the heads of state and the finance ministers since the peak of the recent financial crisis in 2008 has been high by historical standards.

The international monetary governance is pertinent because the growing integration of economies would imply that crisis in a country which is economically important either in a global or in a regional sense would not be confined to the geographical boundaries of the country where the crisis originates. The cross-border issues cover a wide array of subjects that cover the well-known areas of international trade, cross-border banking and financial flows.

In this chapter, we shall discuss the international dimension of monetary governance in the context of the working of the international institutions, in particular the IMF, the committees and groups, and the concerns and perspectives of EMEs on the subject.

The Current Institutional Setting in the International System

The two major multilateral institutions, the IMF and the WB, have been created to address the problems of the post-World War II economies of the world after considerable discussions wherein the major players were the US and the UK.[1] Since then, the two institutions have had amendments to the original Articles of Agreement in response to the changing economic realities. In the case of the IMF, which indeed represents the core institution for functioning of the international monetary and financial system, the first major amendment was in the 1960s after the introduction of the special drawing rights (SDRs) and the second one—a major one at that, was after the breakdown of the fixed exchange parity system in the 1970s.[2] The multilateral institutions have boards of governors consisting of finance/planning ministers or governors of central banks. As the boards cannot be in Washington DC on a daily basis, the policy issues are first dealt with by executive boards, representing member countries which as of March 2011 number 187 countries. The IMF executive board has in all 24 chairs representing the entire membership.

The IMF executive board focusses on the issues that are brought before it though it has the power to initiate discussion on issues that it believes are important and have not been covered by the papers put up before it. The papers are prepared by the staff members who in turn are largely guided by the work of the groups and committees that have been formed by the international economic community.

The policy issues that would impact on the international monetary and financial system are the ones with which the IMF

Executive Board grapples with. These issues are referred to by the International Monetary and Financial Committee (IMFC) which has been in existence since 1974. The IMFC was for about 20 years known as the Interim Committee (IC). The IMFC has 24 members reflecting the number of executive directors in the executive board. The IMFC is chaired generally by Minister of Finance elected by the membership. It is responsible for advising and reporting to the board of governors as it manages and shapes the international monetary and financial system. In addition, it deals with issues of global liquidity, transfer of resources to developing countries and proposals of the executive board for amendments to the Articles of Agreement. It meets generally twice a year—once at the time of the annual meetings of the IMF and the WB during the Fall and again in March/April at the time of the Spring. The most important point to note is that the IMFC meetings provide an agenda of work to be done on the issues relating to the international monetary and financial system. The agenda of work is for the succeeding six months and the board's views on the agenda items are considered by the IMFC along with the contemporary issues at the following IMFC meeting. The IMFC views are arrived not by voting but by consensus.

Its sister committee called the Development Committee formed in 1974 has 26 members and has the mandate to focus on issues related to economic development in emerging and developing countries, issues that are in the domain of the World Bank. The membership is confined usually to ministers of finance or development or planning or economy, who together represent the full membership of the IMF and the WB. Its full name is the Joint Ministerial Committee of the Boards of Governors of the Bank and Fund on the Transfer of Real Resources to Developing Countries. Over the years, it has come to deal not only with issues of development and transfer of financial resources but also with trade and global environment issues. It meets twice a year, generally on the day following the day of the meeting of the IMFC.

Of the two, the most interesting one from the point of view of economists and policy analysts is undoubtedly the IMFC meeting which culminates in the issuance of communiques. The communiques and the post-press meets of the chairman of the IMFC along with the heads of the IMF and the WB are analysed threadbare by international observers of the economic and financial scene.

In recent years the deliberations in both the committees have been influenced by the views of two well-known country groupings, namely the G-7 and G-20. The G-7 major industrial countries (Canada, France, Germany, Italy, Japan, United Kingdom and United States) have been holding annual economic summits at the level of the heads of state/government since 1975. The Group has been acting as the main policy coordination group. Since 1987, the G-7 finance ministers and central bank governors have been meeting at least twice a year to monitor world economic developments and assess economic policies. Russia has joined the Group formally in 1997 essentially for political discussions and has become a full participant since 1998, thereby making the G-7 the Group of 8 (G-8). However, the G-7 as well as G-8 summit meetings take place distinctly every year.

The G-7, however, continued to be a dominant group that sets the agenda of work for the IMFC and the WB. This was very much the case till the late 1990s. The Group still sets the agenda to a considerable extent. The G-7 being the group of industrial countries has derived its strength on account of two reasons: (a) together the countries in the group has a majority in the voting of the multilateral institutions and (b) the group has much stronger research and analytical abilities in their respective governments and central banks to focus on issues of importance for the conduct of the international monetary and financial system.

It was when it became apparent that there are emerging market economies that are as important as IEs from the point of view of the international monetary and financial system, there was a recognition that a beginning has to be made to have a new group that includes not only the IEs but also a few other emerging economies. In 1999 the G-20 was formally established. The leadership role of the Group was assumed by the US. Over time, the G-20 has assumed a powerful voice in the debates on economic and financial matters at the international level. It became an important forum for international economic cooperation since 2008 at the peak of the global economic and financial crisis. The Group has therefore spent considerable time discussing policy issues of IEs and EMEs relating to international financial stability, international liquidity, capital flows, debt sustainability and currency developments, among others.

The formation of G-20 has taken the wind out of the sails of the developing countries' group known as G-24 which was established in 1971 as a chapter of the G-77 that was set up at the end of the first session of the United Nations Conference on Trade and Development (UNCTAD) in Geneva. The G-24 (The Intergovernmental Group of Twenty-Four on International Monetary Affairs and Development) is provided with secretariat services by the IMF. It meets usually twice a year, prior to the meetings of the IMFC and Development Committee. Its membership is limited to 24 countries but all members of the G-77 can take part in the discussions of the Group. China has been a special invitee since 1981.[3] In the first three decades of its existence, it has had very limited support of academic thinkers, among whom the prominent were Sydney Dell, G.K. Helleiner and Dani Rodrik. But in recent years, it received considerable and wider academic support partly on account of the liberal material support of the UNCTAD. Its technical discussion papers present a viewpoint that could be considered as possible alternatives to the G-7 views.

It is important to note here that four countries which are members of G-24, namely, Argentina, India, Mexico and South Africa are also members of G-20. To this may be added China which has the status of special invitee of G-24. Together, these five countries are expected to provide an interesting inter-group feedback mechanism. However, there is not much of evidence of the impact of the feedback on the viewpoints expressed by EME members in G-20 meetings.

The Relative Economic Strength of EMEs and Developing Economies in the Global Economy

The relative economic strength of economies is reflected in the quotas of member countries in the IMF. Voting in the executive board is governed by the quota system. The G-20 group of countries that includes European Union has a sizeable proportion of total quotas. The eight G-20 industrial countries of the Group—Australia, Canada, France, Germany, Italy, Japan, United Kingdom and United States—command 46.77 per cent of the total quotas. The rest of the IEs (including Israel which generally votes with the IE group) have 13.75 per cent of the total quotas. Together, the IEs thus have 60.52 per cent of the total quotas. In terms of votes, they command 57.88 per cent of the total votes.

On the other hand, the EME members of the G-20—Argentina, Brazil, China, India, Indonesia, Korean Republic, Mexico, Russia, Saudi Arabia, South Africa and Turkey—command only 19.78 per cent of the quota and 19.01 per cent of the total votes. Excluding the European Union, the G-20 members as a whole own 66.55 per cent of the total quotas. This translates to 63.43 per cent of the total quotas. This will mean the rest of the world has only 33.45 per cent of the total quotas and 36.57 per cent of the total votes. These numbers suggest the critical economic power that G-20 as a group can wield, if it so wants, for taking decisions that would have profound influence on the conduct of international monetary and financial system.[4]

Effectively speaking, the voting power is exercised by the executive directors on the executive board. In the IMF, 8 executive directors represent only their own countries. The rest of the total number of 24 executive directors represents clusters of countries, referred to as constituencies. While 5 countries' executive directors (of the US, Japan, Germany, France and the UK) are nominated by the countries concerned, the rest are elected. Three executive directors who represent only their countries (China, Saudi Arabia and Russian Federation) are also deemed to have been elected by the countries in question. As at the end of the IMF's fiscal year (ending April 30, 2011), the total voting power of the 5 nominated executive directors amounted to 37.48 per cent of the total votes. The three executive directors who represent single-country constituencies command 9.03 per cent of the total votes, with China alone having 3.82 per cent of the total votes. The remaining executive directors thus have 53.49 per cent of the total votes. Among them, the executive directors who are drawn generally from the country whose share is dominant in the votes of their constituencies are Belgium, Netherlands, Italy, Australia, Canada, India, Brazil and Argentina. The executive directors representing the constituencies headed by Belgium, Netherlands, Italy, Australia and Canada (IEs) command, in all, 20.92 per cent of the total votes. This means that the executive directors representing IEs have 58.42 per cent of the total votes, a commanding majority that can hold sway in most executive board decisions.[5] What is also pertinent to note is that even though European Union (EU) had been formed quite some years ago, there are more than one executive director to represent the EU countries. On the other hand, there are only two executive directors to represent the countries in the entire continent of Africa with only few exceptions, the exceptions being Egypt, Libya, Algeria, Ghana, Morocco and Tunisia.

The IMF decision-making structure was the topic of many a debate on IMF reforms (Truman, 2006 and 2009; Bryant, 2008 and 2010). The debates were made in various country groups. The G-20 in fact discussed the reform of the governance of the IMF and the WB at the London Summit of April 2009 and again at the Pittsburgh Summit of September 2009. These discussions were reflected in the discussions on quotas in the IMF's executive board deliberations. The 14th General Review of Quotas in the fund which was agreed upon in November 2010, however, belied the expectations of EMEs. The review hardly gave sense to sound governance overhaul, notwithstanding the fact that there will be some shift in quota shares in favour of emerging market and developing countries and some protection of the quota shares and voting power of the poorest members. These changes will come into effect towards the end of 2012.

The changes that have been ultimately agreed to mean very little. Advanced economies as a whole will lose 2.8 per cent of their combined quote share from 60.5 per cent as in April 2008 to 57.7 per cent with the conclusion of the 14th General Review of Quotas in 2010. The largest gainers among the IEs are the US, Japan and Spain. China will gain the maximum of 2.4 percentage points over the April 2008 level followed by Brazil of 0.53 percentage points, India of 0.31 percentage points, and Mexico of 0.35 percentage points. Russia will gain only marginally. Saudi Arabia will have some erosion in its share.

The actual reforms proposed and ultimately agreed to in the IMF and the final 14th General Review of Quotas in 2010 hardly mirror the economic realities after the global economic and financial crisis of 2007-2009. There is a strong and widespread view that the quota formulae that have been used so far are flawed since they do not reflect economic realities. Take for example the GDP of nations which is one of the variables in the formula equation. For inter-country comparisons, the GDP of countries which are expressed in national currencies will have to be converted into one widely accepted unit. That unit conventionally was a common currency at market exchange with a weight of 30 per cent even though real growth can be best measured only when GDP data of all countries are converted in terms of purchasing power parity (PPP) (see Virmani and Patra, 2011). If PPP is used, many EMEs will gain, and some of them enormously. However, IEs did not want to have a radical redistribution of quota shares but had agreed to have a blend of market exchange rates and exchange rates based on PPP in a proportion that gives lower weight to the latter. The blend GDP as a concept has no real merit. In fact one could go to the extent of saying that international economic realities would be best reflected by not only making use of GDP (PPP) shares in world aggregate GDP, but also including the world's poor living in different countries so that they would reflect the true 'voice' (Virmani, 2011). If one were to use GDP by PPP, the relative size of the first 10 countries of the world would in the descending order be as follows: US, China, Japan, India, Germany, Russia, UK, France, Brazil and Italy. The next five countries would be: Mexico, Korea, Spain, Canada and Indonesia. China, India, Russia and Brazil—the four BRIC countries—will be in the first 10 of the world by this reckoning.

The institutional governance has so far been inadequate in that the IEs still dominate the proceedings despite the fact that there is a shift in economic power from them to EMEs. As a result, the international community has lost the opportunity of laying down a rule that the relative economic strength of member countries would be measured in a correct and transparent manner every five years without being ideologically or emotionally attached to any particular formulae. Such a rule would have been consistent with the idea of symmetry of treatment of members, an idea that is applied very routinely as a principle in the deliberations of conditionality attached to credit extensions to developing country members in need through a variety of arrangements such as the stand-by and extended fund facility.

Other Governance Issues

The quota system can be only one aspect of the reform of the international monetary and financial system. The policies of the multilateral institutions as well as the governing rules may need to be revisited and amendments made, where necessary. The multilateral institutions as they are presently structured do not have legitimacy. Nor is there observance of the principle of subsidiarity which would hold well if decisions are taken at the lowest level in the international governance system. The governance principles required to be applied for multilateral institutions for enhanced accountability have not been explicitly laid down as yet. Till such a stage is reached, one may have to settle for the second best in that the existing groups and committees should be first subjected to reform process based on the principles of governance, namely universality, legitimacy, subsidiarity and accountability, without any discrimination or asymmetry of treatment of countries.

There is a view that the establishment of G-20 and the actions of the G-20 has provided a measure of legitimacy to IMF. This is based on the belief that without the G-20 support, the IMF would have to depend on friendly countries to increase its resources, the size of its packages and the allocations of SDRs (see Wyplosz, 2009). This belief is not without validity though this has raised a number of other questions. These questions have to do with: (a) the consistency in the membership of G-20 and the IMFC and (b) the very size and inclusiveness of the membership of the G-20 (Eichengreen, 2009; Pohlmann *et al.*, 2010).

The multilateralism practised by the G-20 and the size of the problem could itself be a problem. First there are questions whether G-20 is unwieldy in that it is more of a crowd than smaller groups. On the other hand, there is also a view that it could be enhanced to G-22 or a 'new' G-24 (not to be confused with the G-24 that emerged from the G-77). Eichengreen (2009) in fact argued that it is unwieldy and the Group is ill-suited for putting out fires. He also felt that if the membership in the G-20 and IMFC should be consistent, the G-20 may have to be expanded to 24. Second, there is the question of appropriateness of representation of all the continents or contiguous geographical areas. A large part of East Europe and a good part of the continent of Africa is not adequately represented or is unrepresented. Third, its relationship with the UN has been one of unease. This has irked a number of members of the UN so much so that the President of the UN General Assembly convened a panel of experts, chaired by Joseph Stiglitz in 2009.[6] The Stiglitz group recommendations became the focal point of the UN Conference on the Global Economic Crisis at the end of June 2009. Fourth, the G-20 pre-empted designs for creating G-13 or G-14 that was favoured by France. There was a general feeling that the US, using its lead position in the designing of the G-20 at the end of the 1990s, chose to reward its allies such as South Korea, Indonesia, Australia, Turkey and Saudi Arabia with membership in the Group. Fifth, there are groupings such as the Global Redesign Initiative sponsored by Qatar, Singapore and Switzerland within the World Economic Forum and the Singapore-driven Global Governance Group (or 3G, as it is called) which reflect the fact that the concerns of small states are not adequately represented by the G-20. The Global Governance Group also seized the opportunity of addressing their concerns to the Secretary General of the UN in March 2010.[7] The countries that form the Global Governance Group are: Singapore, Malaysia, Brunei, the Philippines, Vietnam, Bahrain, Qatar, UAE, Sweden, Belgium, Ireland, Liechtenstein, Monaco, San Marino, New Zealand, Chile, Uruguay, Costa Rica, Guatemala, Panama, Jamaica, Barbados, the Bahamas, Rwanda, Senegal and Botswana. Finally, the opposition to the G-20 was on the ground that it was a union of big countries that will dictate new rules, and this was most explicitly expressed by countries such as Venezuela, Bolivia, Cuba and Nicaragua in 2009 under a group called the G-192 summit.[8]

These ideas suggest that while G-20 has so far been able to carry its weight in the discussions on the international monetary and financial system, it has to be seen as objective and sensitive. Objectivity will be visible only if EMEs that are not represented in the G-20 and the developing countries are convinced that the EME members in the Group are not overwhelmed by the views of the IEs in the Group. Sensitivity to the aspirations and expectations of those excluded from the G-20 is essential if G-20 should be seen as credible.

There have also been some suggestions for lowering the voting threshold on most important decisions of the executive board in the IMF. The suggestion was essentially to reduce the threshold from 85 per cent to 70-75 per cent as well as extension of the double majorities to a few other decisions.[9] A number of writers also came out with suggestions to expand the role of SDRs by asking the G-20 governments to commit themselves to the positive consideration of annual and substantial SDR allocations to meet the demands of the members for international reserves without exasperating global imbalances (Truman, 2009 and Bossone, 2010). There was also a suggestion that the IMF Articles regarding capital account policies of members be amended to allow for flexibility (Truman, 2009). A further suggestion by the Palais Royal Initiative (2010) was that the IMFC could well be merged with the G-20 for improving the legitimacy and for providing credible strength to the decisions of the executive board.

It is important to recognise that while the existing multilateral institutions and their operational bye-laws and rules need to be subject to reforms, they will not by themselves ensure that international monetary and financial governance will be secure and that the international community will receive all the 'services' that it requires from a well-functioning international system. There are still a number of issues that need to be resolved through dialogues and institutional arrangements at the international level. A few examples could be provided here for a more careful and overarching reflection, as so well brought out by Bradlow (2011). Monetary regulation, regulation of trade and investment in financial services, regulation of cross-border activities, coordination of national financial regulation, coordinated taxation of financial transactions, arrangements for dealing with sovereign debt problems and complex cross-border bankruptcies, and regulation of international money laundering are some of the areas where much more sharp governance mechanisms and arrangements are necessary. So far there has been no agreement on all these aspects. The only area where some agreement has been reached is in respect of the need for nations to secure financial stability through some consistent application of Basle norms in respect of financial regulation. The Financial Stability Board which is at the forefront of Basle initiatives does not include all the members of the IMF/WB at least as of 2011 and to that extent its legitimacy itself is under some cloud.

The Message

While the listing of the areas of concern for governance arrangements does highlight the issues that need to be resolved for more efficient international monetary governance, there is in the first instance a need for a commitment on the part of the governments of all systemically important countries and in particular of IEs to ensure that the financial and economic imbalances of the kind that have developed since 2007 due to neglect of the regulatory institutions to obtain full compliance of all standards from the market participants and due to insufficient appreciation of the fiscal sustainability issues within their own countries would not recur. It is only when national governments show to the rest of the world that their commitments are adhered to in letter and spirit will the existing arrangements and mechanisms to address the concerns of international community be improved upon.

The current efforts at reaching some agreements in G-20 on some of the issues mentioned above are important even though there is no certainty that the final outcomes will be close to the initial expectations. This is partly because monetary governance at the international level encompasses issues that fall in the domain of a complex policy-mix and institutional arrangements. A number of questions arise as to whether decisions should be taken on the basis of majority view in any group or any institution and whether the decisions are optimal by some recognised criteria. Again, should civil society organisations (CSOs) be allowed to have a say in the matter? If so, which CSOs could be considered as truly representative of international public opinion and aspirations?

Whatever be the final arrangements, they are bound to be informal since national legislative bodies would not easily give legal approvals on the fear that the sovereignty in decision-making will be seen to have been compromised. Yet, it is important to be pragmatic enough to realise that the international community has to work towards improvements in the functioning of the international monetary and financial system through the existing institutions or through somewhat improved arrangements within the institutions and groups. And countries which have larger say in matters would be the ones with relatively strong economies and economies with high potential. All one can do in the circumstances is to strive to improve transparency in the functioning of all the international institutions and country groups and to ensure that they coordinate their activities for the common good across countries.

End Notes

1. See the official history of the IMF brought out by Horsefield and de Vries (1986). Also see Vasudevan (2010) for India's relations with the multilateral institutions in the first 50 years of the existence of the Brettonwood institutions.
2. An excellent account of the discussions undertaken in the IMF was provided by de Vries (1986) and (1987) in her monumental works on the history of the IMF.

3. Its membership consists of Algeria, Argentina, Brazil, Colombia, Democratic Republic of Congo, Cote d'Ivoire, Egypt, Ethiopia, Gabon, Ghana, Guatemala, India, Iran, Lebanon, Mexico, Nigeria, Pakistan, Peru, the Philippines, South Africa, Sri Lanka, Syria, Trinidad and Tobago and Venezuela. Its origin owes a great deal to Paul Prebisch (1950), whose work on economics of trade and development has influenced many a later day thinkers.

4. Calculations of the votes were made by the author on the basis of the fact sheet on the quotas and votes issued by the International Monetary Fund in October 2011 on its website.

5. See International Monetary Fund (2011a). The percentages worked out here are in relation to the total that actually would amount to 99.80 per cent of the total votes, because the votes of Guinea, Madagascar and Somalia which did not participate in the 2010 Regular Election of Executive Directors were excluded. The total votes of these members amounted to 0.20 per cent of all the votes of the entire membership.

6. Widely known as the Commission on Financial Reforms, the formal name of the Commission was 'Commission of Experts of the President of the UN General Assembly on Reforms of the International Monetary and Financial System'. Its mandate was to reflect on the causes of the crisis, assess its impacts on all countries and suggest adequate responses to avoid its recurrence and restore global economic stability. Its first meeting took place in January 2009, the second in March 2009 and the final one by April 2009.

7. The letter was an official one and can be got from the website of the United Nations: *<http://www.un.org/esa/ffd/events/2010GAWGFC/7/Stmt_Singapore.pdf>*. It was entitled, 'Strengthening the Structure (of the UN) for Interchange among the G-20 and Non-members on 11 March 2010 to UN Secretary General by the Permanent Representative of Singapore' (Document A/64/706).

8. The G-192 Summit was on the financial crisis and international developments. See website: *<http://www.un.org/News/briefings/docs/2009/090710_GAPPres.doc.htm>*

9. Palais Royal Initiative—a Group convened by Michel Camdessus, Alexandre Lamfalussy and Tommaso Padoa-Schioppa. Its report came out in 2011 under the title, "Reform of the International Monetary System: A Cooperative Approach for the Twenty First Century". See website: *<http://www.global-currencies.org/smi/gb/telechar/news/Rapport_Camdessus-integral.pdf>*

6

Logging Off to Move Forward

Good monetary governance either at the national level or at the international level is not possible without human endeavour to commit to and to act for the good of the people at large. No doubt, the good of the people is an inherently subjective notion. Yet, public policies cannot ignore such a notion: they have to in fact be led by what is considered to elevate the state of well-being of the vast sections of the population, if not the entire population, from one point in time to another. In reality, this requires making a judgment of the good scoring over the undesirable or the bad.

Monetary governance at the national level in democratic societies can be quite complex in view of the many business and political interests serving their own goals. This is where governments in power have to be seen to be on the side of the majority of the people, in particular the poor and the vulnerable while announcing their decisions and acting upon them. Complex situations also arise in the case of monetary governance at the international level as well. The effectiveness of international monetary governance depends on how well nations reconcile their seemingly irreconcilable positions on issues that have been discussed in the previous chapter. Nations are known to be generally influenced by national considerations. Sovereign nations are known not to give up their positions however weak they are simply because of the fear that any surrender of their own interests in favour of a position that might well reflect another country's best interests would be perceived as a sign of weakness by domestic stakeholders. It is only now, particularly since 2007, with the high degree of economic and financial integration of nations, that it is recognised that it would not be in national interest to be non-cooperative at the international level.

The basic principles of good monetary governance at both the national and international levels are the same. In the previous chapter, mention was made of legitimacy, transparency, subsidiarity and accountability. These are well known but are at times not fully appreciated. Of these, it is on accountability which is essentially rooted in transparency and information dissemination that emphasis is given. Accountability alone would not be enough. There is also a need to bring about structural reforms, apart from using knowledge-centric information for designing policies that are most relevant for sustainable development. We shall deal with these three aspects here.

Accountability

It is widely accepted that accountability for decisions and actions taken has to permeate all activity areas of the ministries and organisations. Accountability is often 'fixed' at the top level (of minister or secretary of the ministry or central bank governor) when decisions go wrong or when the implementation of decisions is not consistent with what had been implicitly taken as a given. Such an approach is not necessarily the correct one to follow at all times. At times, staff members even those at the secondary and tertiary levels would need to be called to question for not implementing what they are expected to according to the rules of the organisations/ministries. After all, ministers and governors are human and dependent on their colleagues at the lower levels for completing the assigned tasks to everyone's satisfaction according to the rules in vogue. On their own, they could err in making judgments when information available to them is weak or asymmetric or unreliable. Accountability can be particularly tricky when macroeconomic policies are discussed by the government and the central bank representatives. In such situations, governors are at a greater disadvantage, being the appointees of the governments and are often expected to go along with the considerations that may not be strictly in accordance with the received technical analyses of monetary management. They may raise their voices of dissent in the inner chambers of policy formulation but they have to ultimately be team persons. This of course does not mean that there were no instances in the history of central banks when governors had to leave their positions for upholding ideas that are not in line with the views of the fiscal authorities or the heads of the governments. Three examples may be cited in this regard. One related to the resignation of the governor in India, about which very little is known outside, despite a vivid account of the event in the second volume of the history of the Reserve Bank of India in the 1950s (RBI, 1998a). The second event was more recent and it occurred at the time of the German unification in 1991 (Vasudevan, 2003; The German Times for Europe, 2007). The third event was also recent, one that occurred in Thailand at the time of the Asian financial crisis in 1997.[1]

Open conflicts in policy enunciation between the governments and central banks are rare though. There are possibly three reasons why confrontational approaches are not adopted. First, central banks have begun to convey to the public at large the impression of being open and consultative with all stakeholders including the relevant ministries in their approaches to the problems on hand. Secondly, improved institutional mechanisms which were discussed in Chapter 2 have been set in place in many EMEs in both the ministries and central banks. The incentive for setting up mechanisms lay in the fact that it enhances the reputation of being team players for advancing the public good. Thirdly, many EMEs have in recent years begun to place the available policy options to the critical challenges on their websites for public reaction within a certain period of time before firming up their decisions. The approach of seeking outside opinion is believed to help the authorities to get an improved insight into the behaviour of market participants and to reassure the public that their sensitivities and concerns are duly taken on board.

Accountability is not amenable to measurement in concrete terms. Yet, the unmistakable fact is that in democratic societies, governments are accountable to the people. The ministers are accountable to the Parliament, and the legally-based committees. They become answerable to the public when they are faced with questions from the media during their press briefings/conferences. They do not avoid the press for they find an incentive for meeting the press if only to check every now and then the public reaction to the policies that s/he as the minister announces so that s/he could take corrective actions, if needed, for getting re-elected. This may not be the case where ministers are not elected and are appointed to their positions as in presidential forms of governments. In such cases, the score card from the press and television media about the rationale of the announced policy and its implementation would be available to the ministers as well as the president and his office. The minister's own tenure would depend on how the president views the score card and since the president's judgments could be highly subjective, it would be necessary for the minister in a presidential form of government to ensure that her/his policies are reflected in the final policy outcomes.

In the case of central banks, accountability may be seen from two angles: one is legal which means that the central bank governor would have to report to the Government or to the committees appointed by the Government. In some cases which are very rare though, governors are given the cabinet rank in which case, what is applicable to the ministers will be applied also to the case of governors of central banks. In reality, the accountability of central bank faces a simple litmus test: how well the policies are explained to the public at large.

The explanations could come through the statements of policy committees, minutes of such committees or special reports or speeches or special articles or notes as well as other communication devices. Communications, therefore, go beyond mere transmittal of economic data. The explanations will have to be simple so that they would be easily understood.

Many a time in the past, some central banks have tried to provide explanations of their policies in a language that is esoteric and creative, leading to different interpretations. This is resorted to even now in good many cases especially by those central banks that consider themselves autonomous or independent. It is not clear whether central banks deliberately use such creative language in order to protect themselves from any serious charge of neglect or incompetence should economic and financial developments turn out to be different from the initial expectations. There is however little doubt that in the short run, the exercise of autonomy through such creative communications could be in conflict with accountability, giving rise to democratic deficit.

Good communication is critical for building up credibility and personal reputations of the management teams, whether in government or in the central bank. This is particularly so when policy decisions have distributional effects. Both fiscal and monetary policies have distributional effects. It is for this reason central banks cannot focus only on one objective such as price stability or on inflation targetting. The distributional effects necessarily involve social trade-offs (Levy, 1995). In certain cases, monetary policy could have a role in foreign policy when it manipulates exchange rate and wields control over economies that are pegged to its currency. This is akin to the 'beggar thy neighbour' policy that was practised by some countries in the 1930s.

Communication strategies have to also take into account the need for reforming the governance structures within the organisations. This may be called, for want of a better term, the 'inclusive' governing structure. Inclusive structure would not be possible without: (a) building adequate capacity of the staff with high quality training programmes, both in-house and outside; (b) appropriate periodic changes of personnel in different internal committees/groups entrusted with clearly spelt out terms of reference and (c) 'inclusive' representation of different regional, linguistic and economic class interests in the overall staff pattern in countries where such interests are of relevance from the point of view of social harmony. Inclusiveness is necessary as much in EMEs and developing countries as in IEs.

Accountability as indicated earlier is not indivisible. It can be shared in many areas of activity in the organisation, especially in operational areas of activity. It can be at different levels of hierarchy of the staff. It can be set with well-tested operational guidelines and numerically fixed targets or reference indicators with some minimal tolerable deviation from the determined targets/indicators, provided that such deviations are justified.

Knowledge-Centric Information

Monetary governance would have to be fostered by broad-based information base that should at the same time be knowledge-centric. This implies that it is not enough to disseminate high quality information and results of special surveys and convey the analytical base of the policy framework. The information has to provide knowledge to people as to what the policies seek to achieve and how well the policies are people-sensitised. It is in this regard, the authorities are at times handicapped in that they are not in a position to establish with definiteness the channels through which fiscal and monetary policies are transmitted to what people desire as their objectives which the authorities translate into targets. This is partly because of the frequent changes in behavioural relationships in the domestic economy. These changes have to do with constant mapping of expectations about the economy and about the available policy options that have a bearing on consumption and investment outcomes. In addition, in a highly integrated world, transmission mechanisms are subject to considerable shocks from outside, leading to adjustments of domestic policies that are contrary to the initially projected policy paths. This was very evident during the recent global financial crisis when the conventionally understood transmission mechanisms did not work and could not therefore be taken as permanently given. This kind of situation could arise even when crisis is not present. Global integration of economies dictates the need for the authorities to revisit periodically the theme of transmission mechanism and design and to implement policies that respond to the evolving economic circumstances. To gain credibility and own accountability, the evolved policies and implementation arrangements should be subjected to impact evaluations, the results of which may be widely conveyed to the public at large. This approach is more robust than making mere announcements of forward guidance policies, a practice that seems to be gaining ground in some central banks of IEs and in some EMEs. Forward guidance policy is expected to signal what the policy stance would be in the near future on an assured basis for a specified period of time. Often it is in the nature of making announcement of continuance of the existing 'policy stance' for a certain specified period of time. But it is not as yet clear as to whether such announcements or statements amount to signalling and whether they will in any way help realise the objective of the current policy action. It would not be totally out of character for transparency-seeking authorities to spring an element of surprise, particularly when the public policy preferences and market preferences are divergent or incongruous.

Adoption of new information technology applications is a common sight in all the governments and central banks of EMEs. They provide knowledge of how economic situations would evolve given the way the main indicator variables have moved in most recent times. For example, high credit growth on a sustained basis may be owing to lax management in banks or expectations of high demand prospects but it also indicates possible default and market risks. Similarly, industrialisation for the sake of exploiting known natural resources may give rise to additional employment but it is not necessarily welfare enhancing if in the process, negative external economies or climatic or ecological disturbances are generated. Information, therefore, has to be imbued with knowledge about the costs and benefits of every public policy initiative and about the future opportunities. In other words, governments and central banks will have to focus not merely on conventional growth and price stability objectives but also on financial stability, climate change and other shocks to real welfare of the society at large. Such information, fortunately, can now be picked up from the websites and could be adapted to the national circumstances.

These instances show the benefits of adopting electronic information management in all areas of the governments and central banks. There are also areas where information management and IT applications help improve economic governance. For example, agro-market information enables farmers to make their choices about the crops to be cultivated and the marketing of crops at the prevailing market prices. Similarly, opening of single-window interface with stakeholders often reduces the costs of red tape and bureaucratic interventions. Again, in central banks, new payment and settlement applications help to transfer funds in quick, almost real time and improve liquidity positions. These in turn reduce volatility in financial markets.

It is necessary to complement information-gathering and dissemination at reasonable costs with information management systems to foster e-governance. In many countries, the right to information has become a part of statute books.[2] Questions are put to governments and central banks seeking information on certain matters of interest to the public. These questions often are conveyed electronically. This right has been apparently playing a critical and important role in the effective functioning of the citizen-centric information system. Such a system will be rendered possible if there is a good governance framework that places emphasis on service delivery. It will also require close collaboration of different departments within the government and on citizens deriving satisfaction from using government services. The satisfaction derived while receiving public services could be heightened if citizens are not merely passive recipients of public services, but also owners and participants in the creation of such services.

In the case of central banks in EMEs, there is a growing emphasis on promoting financial development through actions that enable commercial banks to provide financial inclusion as a part of new e-information and e-governance mechanism.[3] All adults who are eligible to use financial services would then have access to such eligibility. Access is enabled through conventional channels such as expansion of bank branch networks and easing of procedures for availing of banking services at minimal cost as also through new modes such as mobile banking, ATMs, mobile phone banking. In addition to financial inclusion, there are also efforts to give added impetus to the financial regulatory mechanisms through adoption of intense IT applications and management systems, drawing on the experience gained from the supervisory and regulatory concerns and actions of the international community in response to the recent global financial crisis. Most central banks have financial stability units as separate departments or as parts of financial supervision or regulation departments with persons having both theoretical background and operational experience. Financial stability reports are brought out periodically for wider public information. Such institutional mechanisms will have to be set up in central banks all over the world. The reports and the speeches of the central bank management teams will have to be such that they provide important inputs to investors in determining consumption-investment distribution and making portfolio choices.

Structural Reforms

The third important requirement for effective monetary governance has to do with the structural aspects that help to bring about institutional changes. For this purpose, the internal organisation structure should be cohesive and mutually interactive. The functions of each department need to be clearly stated and mechanisms evolved to operate upon the stated functions on a regular basis.

The mechanisms needed to bring about institutional changes could be broadly placed under three heads: (a) structural reforms based on market orientations; (b) evolution of affordable alternative policy options and alternative avenues for development of new markets and (c) reforms to integrate different markets of the domestic economy and domestic markets with international economies. These three areas are not mutually exclusive: they are in fact interactive.

On (a), there is a general notion, not yet firmly tested though, that market oriented economies would mean minimisation of the role of the government and central bank. If there is one aspect that the recent global economic and financial crisis has brought to the fore, it is that the government and central bank have an important and a concerted role to play as promoters and regulators of economic activity. With growing need for establishing financial stability firmly, it has become imperative to ensure that both the domestic and international operations of banks and other financial institutions are closely screened and regulated along with setting up of sound supervisory systems. Regulations do not imply nationalisation or public ownership. They are only enablers of better financial governance. In the process, the corporate governance in all the financial institutions (including commercial banks) will have to be set on firm footing with necessary legal and institutional back-up. This has to do also with the establishment of internal audit committees and rules for conduct of directors on the management boards of all the financial institutions. Structural reforms have to be such as to ensure that governments get information about the operational efficiency of the new institutional mechanisms in place in the financial institutions in order to be compliant with the provisions of the right to information legislations. Central banks (in concert with other financial regulators) need to also have sufficient information for ensuring that the new institutional mechanisms are in line with the regulatory rules and are working well.

Global financial and technological integration requires that national governments and central banks act in concert to have a wide range of regulations to ensure that their national economies as well as the international monetary and financial system do not stagnate or bear too much of adjustment costs. Capital flows for example is one example that could be cited in this regard. Whether this could be regulated by a Tobin-type tax is a question on which the jury is still not out.

On (b), there is a need for undertaking a large scale programme of policy and market research in EMEs whose economic structures are not exactly the same as those found in IEs. Such research has to be rooted in the economic and social realities of the country in question. The tendency to accept the conventional theories emanating from the IEs is giving way in policy circles in many EMEs to adoption of policy initiatives based on the information available from within the domestic economies. This could be seen from the fact that while growth was accepted as a necessary condition for economic progress, policymakers are leaning towards orienting it with social and infrastructure development on a simultaneous footing. The number of poverty and unemployment studies that have been conducted in recent years in many EMEs and initiation of public welfare programmes show that pure growth models have become irrelevant.[4]

On the development of new markets, there is now a realisation that financial stability cannot be sustained unless regulatory framework is quickly set even as new products and new financial markets are being designed in EMEs. For instance, credit default swaps (CDSs) which came under considerable suspicion and were about to be introduced in many EMEs under the weight of opinion in IEs in favour of CDS, are not totally rejected from contention and could well make entry in EMEs some time in future with suitable regulations in place.

On (c), it is erroneous to think that the recent global economic and financial crisis necessarily implies rejection of the ideas of integrating domestic markets and of integrating the domestic and international markets. Markets in reality should be viewed in broad terms to include financial activity, commodities and labour. Trading in commodities across countries and within countries takes place but in so far as international trade is concerned, there are some barriers, both tariff and non-tariff. The WTO takes care of this issue but national interests often come in the way of reaching optimal solutions. Labour market integration across countries is not easy in view of the difficulties in sorting out immigration laws of different governments. It is doubtful if free labour movements across nations would ever be possible. Financial market integration at the international level without appropriate regulation and ready willingness to coordinate both fiscal and financial policies on the part of governments would not lead to the expected efficiency in the functioning of the international monetary and financial system. The G-20, as already discussed, would be involved with this matter in the months to come. Whether the deliberations in the G-20 on this issue would be accepted by the broad-based international community is a matter of conjecture at this point in time. Wider acceptance of the proposals would depend upon how the G-20 would ensure that the potential costs of economic globalisation are non-existent or very negligible. The potential costs could include high degree of concentration of capital flows, and misallocation of flows with adverse effects on growth of domestic economies and on domestic macroeconomic stability.

In so far as domestic financial market integration is concerned, there is little disagreement on the advantages it offers. It helps to serve as a conduit for monetary authorities to transmit important price signals. It also helps to promote savings and investment, assuming that integration is efficient. It also leads to innovation and to cost-minimising financial intermediation. Essentially, most EMEs try to bring about transformation in the structure of markets and to reduce arbitrage opportunities. This can be done through strengthening competition, deepening financial markets with the help of product innovations, easing restrictions on flows as well as transactions and lowering transaction costs. At the same time, EMEs will have to ensure that adequate liquidity is rendered available. In so far as integration with the rest of the world is concerned, EMEs generally go through the route of capital account liberalisation that would be in keeping with macroeconomic developments, the state of readiness of the domestic financial system and the dynamics of international financial markets. One cannot take ideological positions with regard to full capital account convertibility, as the harsh realities suggest, notwithstanding what the theoretical models seem to point out.

Moving Forward

Laws relating to governance and normative observations on how governance should be conducted do not matter in the final analysis. What matters most is information-based action with accountability attached to it. It is important to realise that time is running out for most countries, in particular the EMEs. For, the proportion of younger population in total population is high and on the rise in EMEs and developing countries. The new generations have the new technologies to network and give vent to their inner feelings on to the streets in the form of protests. They need jobs. They also seek economic and social justice. They are increasingly becoming impatient when they do not see public actions in support of the values that they hold as critical for realising sustainable development. The open street demonstrations in some of the parts of Northern Africa and Middle East in 2011 are a testimony to the fact that the values of life where freedom, development and equality are dominant cannot be framed in any ideological prisms. The protest wave will not be confined to any geographical boundary: it will some time or the other shake up the whole world.

One does not need to lose hope. Sound monetary governance applied with a measure of flexibility under certain specified conditions along with strong political commitment to address the current economic problems would still show that there is light at the end of the tunnel. Thus, this is the new space that should be availed of.

End Notes

1. The Governor of the Bank of Thailand in 1997 had to resign when the country was in serious currency crisis owing to large short-term foreign borrowing by banks and finance companies facilitated as it is by large interest rate differentials. The Governor was made the scapegoat even though the Minister of Finance till almost the middle of June 1996 seemed to help revamp the financial sector by suspending the weak finance companies along with the Governor. However, the coalition politics did not allow the Minister to implement his plans. Defending the exchange rate with large interventions did not work in view of the growing erosion of confidence in the Thai baht and the growing current account deficits. The Governor had to resign as he had no support from the new political masters. His resignation coincided with the arrival of the IMF team in Bangkok to work out strategies to meet the crisis. For an understanding of the political economy aspect of the Asian financial crisis, see Haggard and MacIntyre (2003).

2. The right to information or freedom of information legislations exist in a number of countries. As of now 85 countries have implemented some form of such legislation. India's Right to Information Act was passed in 2005. In Nigeria, the Freedom of Information Bill was signed by the President in February 2011.

3. See NABARD (2008) and Chakrabarty (2011) for a comprehensive account on financial inclusion.

4. Studies on poverty have been plenty. For a simple account of the definitions of poverty, see Spicker (2007), also see Maxwell (1999). For the employment opportunities provided on a mandated basis, see Government of India (2005). For a review of the Act, see Agarwal (2010).

References

Abiad, A. and Jonathan D. Ostry (2005). "Primary Surpluses and Sustainable Debt Levels in Emerging Market Countries", *IMF Policy Discussion Paper* No. 05/6, Washington DC, International Monetary Fund.

Agarwal, Harsh (2010). "National Rural Employment Guarantee Act—A Review", from the website: *<http://www.policyproposals forindia.com/print_article.php?article_id=169& languageid=1>*

Akerlof, G.A. (1970). "The Market for Lemons: Qualitative Uncertainty and the Market Mechanism", *Quarterly Journal of Economics* 84: 488-500.

Bagehot, Walter (1873). *Lombard Street: A Description of the Money Market.* London. William Clowes and Sons. Reproduced in Volume 9 of *The Collected Works of Walter Bagehot*, edited by Norman St. John-Stevas, London, *The Economist*, 1978.

*Bailey, M.J. (1956). "The Welfare Costs of Inflationary Finance", *Journal of Political Economy* 64: 93-110.

*Banerjee, Abhijit (1992). "A Simple Model of Herd Behavior", *Quarterly Journal of Economics* 107: 797-817.

Bank for International Settlements (2010). *Annual Report* (No. 80), June.

———. (2009). "Communication of Monetary Policy Decisions by Central Banks: What is Revealed and Why", *BIS Papers* No. 47.

Bank of England (2008). "The Development of the Bank of England's Market Operations", See *<http://www.bankofengland.co.uk>*

———. (2011). "Recent Developments in the Sterling Monetary Framework", Speech given by Paul Fisher, Executive Director, Manchester Economics Seminar, University of Manchester, March 30, 2011. See *<http://www.bankofengland.co.uk/publications/speeches>*

Barro, R.J. (1982). "Measuring the Fed's Revenue from Money Creation", *Economic Letters* 10: 327-32.

Barro, R.J. and D.B. Gordon (1983). "A Positive Theory of Monetary Policy in a Natural Rate Model", *JPE* 91: 589-610.

Barth, J.R., G. Caprio and Ross Levine (2006). *Rethinking Banking Regulation: Till Angels Govern.* New York: Cambridge University Press.

Bebczuk, R. (2003). *Asymmetric Information in Financial Markets: Introduction and Applications.* Cambridge: Cambridge University Press.

Bergr, Helge, Volker Nitsch and T. Libek (2008). "Central Bank Boards around the World: Why Does Membership Size Differ", *European Journal of Political Economy* 24: 817-32.

Bergr, Helge and Volker Nitsch (2008). "Enough is Enough: How Many People Should Decide about Monetary Policy", May. See *http://www.voxeu.org/index.php?q+node/1181*

Bernanke, Ben S. (2009). "The Crisis and the Policy Response", Stamp Lecture, London School of Economics, London, January 13. This article can be obtained from the Federal Reserve System's website at: *http://www.federalreserve.gov/newsevents/speech/bernanke20090113a.htm*

*Bernanke, Ben S. and M. Gertler (1995). "Inside the Black Box: The Credit Channel of Monetary Policy Transmission", *Journal of Economic Perspectives* 9: 27-48.

———. (1990). "Financial Fragility and Economic Performance", *Quarterly Journal of Economics* 105: 87-114.

Bernanke, Ben S., Thomas Laubach, F.S. Mishkin and A.S. Posen (1999). *Inflation Targeting: Lessons from the International Experience.* Princeton: Princeton University Press.

Bernanke, Ben S. and F.S. Mishkin (1997). "Inflation Targeting: A New Framework for Monetary Policy", *Journal of Economic Perspectives* 11(2): 97-116.

Bernhardsen, Tom and Arne Kloster (2010). "Liquidity Management System: Floor or Corridor?", *Staff Memo* No. 4, Oslo: Norges Bank.

*Blinder, Alan (2007a). "Leadership in Groups: A Monetary Policy Experiment", *CEPS Working Paper* 151.

———. (2007b). "On the Design of Monetary Policy Committees", *CEPS, Working Paper* 153.

*Blinder, Alan and John Morgan (2005). "Are Two Heads Better than One? Monetary Policy by Committee", *Journal of Money, Credit and Banking* 37: 789-811.

Blinder, Alan, M. Ehrmann, M. Fratzscher, J. De Haan and D. Jansen (2008). "Central Bank Communication and Monetary Policy: A Survey of Theory and Evidence", *Journal of Economic Literature* 46(4): 910-45.

Blanchard, Olivier, J.C. Choraqui, R.P. Hagemann and N. Sartor (1990). "The Sustainability of Fiscal Policy: New Answers to an Old Question", *OECD Economic Studies* 15.

Bohn, H. (1998). "The Behavior of US Public Debt and Deficits", *Quarterly Journal of Economics* 87.

Bossone, Biagio (2010). "Dear G20 Leaders, We Need Better Governance", November 15. See the website: *<http://www.voxeu.org/index.php?q=node/5793>*

Bradlow, Daniel D. (2011). "A Critical Assessment of the Strategy and Tactics for Reforming Global Financial Governance", September 6. *<http://www.voxeu.org/index.php?q=node/6946.*

Bresciani-Turroni, C. (1937). *The Economics of Inflation: A Study of Currency Depreciation in Post-war Germany.* London: George Allen & Unwin Ltd., (original English edition) Reprinted 2003 by Oxford, UK: Routledge.

Bryant, C. Ralph (2008). *Reform of Quota and Voting Shares in the International Monetary Fund: 'Nothing' is Temporarily Preferable to an inadequate 'Something'.* Washington DC. Brookings Institution. January.

———. (2010). *Governance Shares for the International Monetary Fund: Principles, Guidelines, Current Status.* Washington DC: Brookings Institution.

Buiter, W. (1985). "A Guide to Public Sector Debt and Deficits", *Economic Policy* 1.

Cagan, P. (1956). "The Monetary Dynamics of Hyperinflation", in Milton Friedman (ed.), *Studies in the Quantity Theory of Money.* Chicago IL. Chicago University Press.

Calvo, G.A. (1978). "Optimal Seigniorage from Money Creation: An Analysis in Terms of the Optimum Balance of Payments Deficit Problem", *Journal of Monetary Economics* 4: 503-17.

———. (2003). "Explaining Sudden Stop, Growth Collapse and BoP Crises: The Case of Distortionary Output Taxes", *IMF Staff Papers.*

Calvo, G.A., A. Izquierdo and L. Mejia (2004). "On the Empirics of Sudden Stops: The Relevance of Balance Sheet Effects", *NBER Working Paper* 10520.

Chakrabarty, K.C. (2011). "Financial Inclusion and Banks: Issues and Perspectives", Address given at the FICCI-UNDP Seminar on *Financial Inclusion: Partnership between Banks, MFIs and Communities,* New Delhi, October 14, 2011. Available under the category of Speeches on the website of the Reserve Bank of India. *<http://www.rbi.org.in>*

Chortareas, Georgios E. and Stephen M. Miller (2002). "Central Banker Contracts, Incomplete Information and Monetary Policy Surprises: In Search of a Selfish Central Banker?", University of Connecticut, *Working Papers* 29 in *Public Choice* 116 (3-4): 271-95. Springer.

Cooper, Andrew F. and Eric Helleiner (2010). "The G-20: A Global Economic Government in the Making?", *Friedrich Eberto Stiftung International Policy Analysis,* in the publication of the same name edited by Christoph Pohlmann, Stephan Reichert and Hubert Rene Schillinger, June. On the website: *<http://library.fes.de/pdf-files/id/ipa/07284.pdf>*

Cukierman, A. and A.H. Meltzer (1986). "A Positive Theory of Discretionary Policy, the cost of Democratic Government and the Benefits of a Constitution", *Economic Inquiry* 24: 367-88.

Currie, Elizabeth, Jean-Jacques Dethier and Eriko Togo (2003). "Institutional Arrangements for Public Debt Management", *World Bank Policy Research Working Paper* 3021.

de Vries, Margaret (1986). *The International Monetary Fund, 1972-1978: Cooperation on Trial.* Washington DC: International Monetary Fund.

———. (1987). *The International Monetary Fund, 1966-1971: The System Under Stress.* Washington DC: International Monetary Fund.

Dincer, Nergiz and B. Eichengreen (2009). "Central Bank Tansparency: Causes, Consequences and Updates", *NBER Working Papers* 14791.

*Dixit, Avinash K. (2003). "On Modes of Economic Governance", *Econometrica* 71: 449-81.

———.* (2004). *Lawlessness and Economics: Alternative Modes of Governance.* Princeton, NJ: Princeton University Press.

———. (2009). "Governance Institutions and Economic Activity", *American Economic Review* 99: 5-24. Presidential Address to the American Economic Association, January.

———.* (1996). *The Making of Economic Policy.* Cambridge: The MIT Press.

Domar, Evsey (1944). "The Burden of the Debt and the National Income", *American Economic Review* 34. December.

ECB (2008). *The Implementation of Monetary Policy in the Euro Area, General Documentation on Eurosystem Monetary Policy Instruments and Procedures.* See <*http://www.ecb.org*>

Edwards, S. (2005). "Capital Controls, Sudden Stops and Current Account Reversals", *NBER Working Paper* 11170.

Eichengreen, Barry (2009). "The G20 and the Crisis", March 2. On the website: <*<http://www.voxeu.org/index.php?q=node/3160*

Eichengreen, Barry, P. Gupta and A. Mody (2006). "Sudden Stops and IMF-supported Programs", *NBER Working Paper* 12235.

Engert, W., T. Gravell and D. Howard (2008). "The Implementation of Monetary Policy in Canada", *Discussion Paper* 2008/9. See *<http://www.bankofcanda.ca*

Fischer, Stanley (1982). "Seigniorage and the Case for a National Money", *Journal of Political Economy* 90: 295-313. April.

*Fratianni, M., J. Hagen and Christopher Waller (1997). "Central Banking as a Political Principal-agent Problem", *Economic Inquiry* 35: 378-93. April.

Friedman, M. (1960). *A Program for Monetary Stability.* NY: Fordham University Press.

———.* (1956). "The Quantity Theory of Money: A Restatement", in M. Friedman (ed.), *Studies in the Quantity Theory of Money.* Chicago: University of Chicago Press.

———.* (1968). "The Role of Monetary Policy", *American Economic Review* 58: 1-17.

———.* (1970). "A Theoretical Framework for Monetary Analysis", *Journal of Political Economy* 78: 193-238.

———. (1971). "Government Revenue from Inflation", *Journal of Political Economy* 79: 846-56. July/August.

Fujiki, Hiroshi (2005). "The MPC and the Incentive Problem, A Selective Survey", *IMES Discussion Paper* No. E-4, Institute for Monetary and Economic Studies, Bank of Japan, Japan.

Gerling, Kerstein, Hans Peter Guner, Alexandra Kiel and Elisabeth Schulte (2005). "Information Acquisition and Decision Making in Committees: A Survey", *European Journal of Political Economy* 21: 563-97.

Ghosh, A.R., J.I. Kim, E.G. Mendoza, J.D. Ostry and M.S. Qureshi (2011). "Fiscal Fatigue, Fiscal Space and Debt Sustainability in Advanced Economies", *NBER Working Paper* 16782.

Goodhart, Charles E. (2009). "Liquidity Management", Paper presented at the Conference on *Financial Stability and Macroeconomic Policy*, Federal Bank of Kansas City, Jackson Hole, Wyoming. See *http://kcfed.con/publicat/sympos/2009/papers/Goodhart.09-11-09.pdf>*

Government of India (2005). *National Rural Employment Guarantee Act*, The Gazette of India, Extraordinary, Part II, Section 1, No. 48, September 07, New Delhi.

Grossman, S.G. (1983). "An Analysis of the Principal-agent Problem", *Econometrica* 51: 1-39.

Haggard, Stephen and Andrew MacIntyre, "The Political Economy of the Asian Financial Crisis", available from website: *<http://igcc3.ucsd.edu/pdf/afc/afc_haggard.pdf>*. This article must have appeared before 2003 since it was cited in 2003 in one of the articles on a similar theme.

Harris, M. and A. Raviv (1979). "Optimal Incentive Contracts with Imperfect Information", *Journal of Economic Theory* 20: 231-59.

*Holmstrom, Bengt and Paul Milgroom (1991). "Multi-task Principal-Agent Analyses: Incentive Contracts, Asset Ownership and Job Design", *Journal of Law, Economics and Organization* 7(sp 1): 24-52.

Hochreiter, Eduard and Riccardo Rovelli (2001). "The Generation and Distribution of Central Bank Seigniorage in the Czech Republic, Hungary and Poland", from the website: *http://www.jvi.org/fileadmin/jvi-files/Eduard_Hochreiter/EH-2001-3.pdf*

Horsefield, J. Keith and Margaret Garritsen de Vries (1986). *The International Monetary Fund, 1945-1965: Twenty Years of International Co-operation.* Washington DC: International Monetary Fund.

International Monetary Fund (2008). "Reform of IMF Quotas and Voice: Responding to Changes in the Global Economy", *Issues Brief*, April/040108.

———. (2010a). *Fact Sheet: IMF Quotas*, November. See website: *http://www.imf.org/external/np/exr/facts/quotas.htm*

———. (2010b). "IMF Quota and Governance Reform: Elements of an Agreement", *IMF Policy Paper*, (103110) October 31.

———. (2011a). *Annual Report*, Appendix IV, Washington DC.

———. (2011b). *World Economic Outlook*. Washington DC: International Monetary Fund, September.

International Monetary Fund and World Bank Staff Paper (2003). *Guidelines for Public Debt Management*. Washington DC.

———. (2007). *Strengthening Debt Management Practices, Lessons from Country Experiences and Issues Going Forward.*

Johnson, Harry G. (1969). "A Note on Seigniorage and the Social Saving from Substituting Credit for Commodity Money", in Robert A. Mundell and Alexander K. Swoboda (eds.), *Monetary Problems of the International Economy*. Chicago IL: Chicago University Press.

Kahn, George A. (2007). "Communicating a Policy Path: The Next Frontier in Central Bank Transparency?", *Economic Review* Q 1: 25-51. Federal Reserve Bank of Kansas City.

———. (2010). "Monetary Policy Under a Corridor Operating Framework", *Economic Review* Q 4: 5-34. Federal Reserve Bank of Kansas City.

Klein, M. and M.J.M. Neumann (1990). "Seigniorage: What is it and Who gets it?", *Weltwirtschaftliches Archiv*, Heft 2: 205-21.

Kopits, George (2001). "Fiscal Rules: Useful Policy Framework or Unnecessary Ornament?", *Working Paper* No. 145, Washington DC, International Monetary Fund.

Kydland, F. and Edward Prescott (1977). "Rules Rather than Discretion: The Inconsistency of Optimal Plans", *Journal of Political Economy* 85: 472-91.

Laeven, L. and Ross Levine (2007). "Is There a Diversification Discount in Financial Conglomerates", *Journal of Financial Economics* 85: 331-67.

Levine, Ross (2011). "Regulating Finance and Regulators to Promote Growth", FRB of Kansas City Conference, Jackson Hole, Wyoming, August 2011.

Levy, David A. (1995). "Does Independent Central Bank Violate Democracy?", *The Jerome Levy Economics Institute Working Paper* No. 148, Levy Economics Institute of Bard College, Annandale-on-Hudson, New York.

Mankiw, N.G. (1986). "The Allocation of Credit and Financial Collapse", *Quarterly Journal of Economics* 101: 405-70.

Maxwell, Simon (1999). "Poverty Briefing", download from: *<http://www.odi.org.uk/resources/download/2277.pdf>*

Mishkin, Frederic S. (1995). "Symposium on the Monetary Transmission Mechanism", *Journal of Economic Perspectives* 9(4): 3-10. Fall.

———. (2000). "What Should Central Banks Do?", *Federal Reserve Bank of St Louis Review* 82(6): 1-14.

———. (2002). "The Role of Output Stabilization in the Conduct of Monetary Policy", *International Finance* 5: 213-27.

Mohan, Rakesh (2005). "Communications in Central Banks: A Perspective", See under speeches of the Reserve Bank of India website, <*http://www.rbi.org.in*>

Mohanty, Deepak (2011). "How Does the Reserve Bank of India Conduct Its Monetary Policy?", See <*http://www.rbi.org.in*> under "speeches". Delivered on August 12, 2011 at Lucknow.

Montiel, P. and C. Reinhart (1999). "Do Capital Controls and Macroeconomic Policies Influence the Volume and Composition of Capital Flows? Evidence from the 1990s", *Journal of International Money and Finance* 18: 619-35.

NABARD (2008). *Report of the Committee on Financial Inclusion (2008).* (Chairman: C. Rangarajan), Mumbai.

Nawrath, Axel (2000). *The Task Group on Incentives to Foster Implementation of Standards and Codes.* Financial Stability Forum (currently Financial Stability Board), Bank for International Settlements, Basle (Available at the website of the BIS).

Patel, I.G. (2002). *Glimpses of Indian Economic Policy—An Insider's View.* New Delhi: Oxford University Press.

*Poluha, Eva and Mona Rosendahl (ed.) (2002). *Contesting 'good' Governance: Cross Cultural Perspectivs on Representation, Accountability and Public Space.* London: Routledge Curzon.

Poole, W. (1970). "Optimal Choice of Monetary Policy Instruments in a Simple Stochastic Macro Model", *Quarterly Journal of Economics* 100: 1169-89.

Prati, A. and M. Sbracia (2002). "Currency Crises and Uncertainty About Fundamentals", *IMF Working Paper* 3, Washington DC.

Prebisch, Paul (1950). *The Economic Development of Latin America and Its Principal Problems.* New York: United Nations.

*Premchand, A. (2010). *Contemporary India: Society and Its Governance.* New Brunswick (USA and London, UK). Transactions Publishers.

Quiros, Gabriel Perez and Hugo Rodriguez Mendizabal (2009). "Asymmetric Standing Facilities: An Unexploited Monetary Policy Tool", *Barcelona Economics Working Paper* No. 414, pp.1-30.

Rangarajan, C. (1993). "Autonomy of Central Bank", Tenth Kutty Memorial Lecture, Calcutta, September, *Mimeo.*

Rangarajan, C., Anupam Basu and Narendra Jadhav (1989). "Dynamics of Interaction between Government Deficit and Domestic Debt in India", *RBI Occasional Papers* 10(3): September.

*Reddy, Y.V. (2011). *Global Crisis, Recession and Uneven Recovery.* Hyderabad: Orient Blackswan (P) Limited.

Reserve Bank of India (1970). *Reserve Bank of India, 1935-51.* Mumbai, India.

———. (1998a). *Reserve Bank of India, 1951-67.* Mumbai, India.

———. (1998b). *Annual Report, 1997-98.* Mumbai, India.

———. (2006). *Reserve Bank of India, 1967-81.* Mumbai, India.

———. (2010). "Challenges to Central Banking in the Context of Financial Crisis", First International Research Conference on Mumbai, India, February 12-13, 2010. For the papers presented therein, see website: <*http://www.rbi.org.in*>

*Rodrik, Dani (2007). *One Economics: Many Recipes—Globalization, Institutions and Economic Growth.* Princeton: Princeton University Press.

Rogoff, Kenneth (1985). "The Optimal Degree of Commitment to an Intermediate Target", *Quarterly Journal of Economics* 100(4): 1169-89.

*Salamon, Lester M. (ed.) (2002). *The Tools of Government: A Guide to the New Governance.* New York: Oxford University Press.

Sheng, Andrew (2000). *The Task Force on Implementation of Standards.* Financial Stability Forum (presently Financial Stability Board), Bank for International Settlements, Basle. Available at the Bank's website.

———.* (2009). *From Asian to Global Financial Crisis—An Asian Regulator's View of Unfettered Finance in the 1990s and 2000s.* Cambridge, UK: Cambridge University Press.

Spence, M. (1973). "Job Market Signalling", *Quarterly Journal of Economics* 87: 355-74.

———. (1974). *Market Signalling.* Cambridge, Mass.: Harvard University Press.

Spicker, Paul (2007). "Definitions of Poverty: 12 Clusters of Meaning", download from: *<http://rszarf.ips.edu.pl/welfare-state/spicker.pdf>*

Spilimbergo, A., S. Symanski, Olivier J. Blanchard and C. Cottarelli (2008). "Fiscal Policy for the Crisis", *IMF Staff Position Note* 08/01.

Stiglitz, Joseph E. (1987). "Principal Agent", in *The New Palgrave—A Dictionary of Economics* 3: 966-71.

Stiglitz, Joseph E. and A. Weiss (1981). "Credit Rationing in Markets with Imperfect Information", *American Economic Review* 71: 393-410.

Subba Rao, D. (2011). "Central Bank Governance Issues: Some RBI Perspectives", Comments made at the meeting of the Central Bank Governance Group in Basel on May 09. This may be read on the RBI website under the category of Speeches at: *http://www.rbi.org.in*

Svensson, Lars E.O. (1999). "Inflation Targeting as a Monetary Policy Rule", *NBER Working Paper* 6790; Also *Journal of Monetary Economics* 43: 607-54.

———. (2005). "Monetary Policy with Judgment: Forecast Targeting", *International Journal of Central Banking* 1(1): 1-54.

———. (2010). "Inflation Targeting after the Financial Crisis", Paper presented at the Reserve Bank of India's First International Research Conference on *Challenges to Central Banking in the Context of Financial Crisis.* See *BIS Review* 16/2010. *http://www.bis.org/review/r100216d.pdf?frames=0*

*Sundararajan, V., Peter Dattels and Hans Blommestein (eds.) (1997). *Coordinating Public Debt and Monetary Management.* Washington DC: International Monetary Fund.

Taylor, John B. (1993). "Discretion versus Policy Rules in Practice", *Carnegie-Rochester Conference Series on Public Policy* 39: 195-214.

———.* (1995). "The Monetary Transmission Mechanism: An Empirical Framework", *Journal of Economic Perspectives* 9: 11-26.

———.* (ed.) (1999). *Monetary Policy Rules.* Chicago: University of Chicago Press.

———. (2000). "Reassessing Discretionary Fiscal Policy", *The Journal of Economic Perspectives* 14(3): 21-36.

———. (2009). "The Lack of an Empirical Rationale for a Revival of Discretionary Fiscal Policy", *American Economic Review* 99(2): 550-55, The Annual Meeting of the American Economic Association Session. May.

The German Times for Europe (July 2007). "Fifty Years of Success", July. Referring to Bundesbank's performance from 1957 and making a reference to the resignation of the President of the Bank on account of differences of views with the Chancellor on terms of the German Unification *<http://www.german-times.comindex.php?option=com_content&task=view&id=863&Itemid=62>*

Truman, Edwin M. (2006). "Rearranging IMF Chairs and Shares: The Sine Qua Non of IMF Reform", in Edwin M. Truman (ed.), *Reforming the IMF for the 21st Century*. Special Report 19, Washington DC, Peterson Institute of International Economics, April.

———. (2009). "The G-20 and International Financial Institution Reform: Unfinished IMF Reform", January 28. See *<http://www.voxeu.org/index.php?q=node/2896>*

*United Nations (2000). *Economic Governance, Guidelines for Effective Financial Management*. NY: United Nations.

Vasudevan, A. (2003). *Central Banking for Emerging Market Economies*. New Delhi: Academic Foundation.

———. (2010). "International Financial Cooperation: India's Interface with the International Monetary Fund and World Bank", in A.B. Sawant (ed.), *Sixty Years of India's Contribution to the United Nations*. New Delhi: Authors Press. This article was originally written in 2005 on the occasion of the 50th anniversary of the UN for an international seminar held in 2006 at Mumbai.

Virmani, Arvind (2011). "Global Economic Governance: IMF Quota Reform", *IMF Working Paper* WP/11/208, July.

Virmani, Arvind and Michael Debabrata Patra (2011). "IMF Reforms 2010: Do They Mirror Global Economic Realities?", *Economic and Political Weekly* XLVI(30): 53-61. Mumbai, July 23.

*Walsh, Carl (1995). "Optimal Contracts for Central Bankers", *American Economic Review* 85: 150-67.

———. (1998). *Monetary Theory and Policy*. Cambridge: The MIT Press (First Edition).

Whitesell, W. (2006). "Interest Rate Corridors and Reserves", *Journal of Economics* 53: 1177-95.

Woodford, Michael (2005). "Central Bank Communication and Policy Effectiveness", *Proceedings*, Federal Reserve Bank of Kansas City. pp. 399-474.

Wolswijk, Guido and Jakob de Haan (2005). "Government Debt Management in the Euro Area—Recent Theoretical Developments and Changes in Practices", *ECB Occasional Paper* No. 24.

Wyplosz, Charles (2009). "Can the G20 reform the international economic system", January 28. Website: *<http://www.voxeu.org/index.php?q=node/2891>*

(Note: The references with asterisk mark are added with the aim of advancing understanding of the arguments made in this book.)

Index